The potato is one of the world's most popular vegetables, as researching this book proved – virtually every country has an identifiable national dish starring potatoes in a leading role. This is certainly true in my house... mash, chips, wedges all loom large on my family's weeknight menu, with more elaborate dishes debuting on the weekend. After you sample all these recipes, I'm sure you'll be intrigued and delighted with the surprising versatility of the humble spud.

Pamela Clark

Food Director

contents

the perfect potato chip

PREPARATION TIME 10 MINUTES (PLUS STANDING TIME) **COOKING TIME** 20 MINUTES

Claimed as pommes frites in France, french fries in America, and chips in Australia and England, the fact remains that this humble fried potato is believed to have been invented by the Belgians. What everyone agrees on is that a perfect chip has to be long, crunchy, golden-brown and possess an earthy, rustic taste enlivened with a hint of oil. Russet burbank (also known as an idaho potato in many cookbooks), with its floury texture and low moisture content, makes the perfect chip, but you can also use bintje or spunta.

1kg russet burbank potatoes, peeled
peanut oil, for deep-frying

1 Cut potatoes lengthways into 1cm slices; cut each slice lengthways into 1cm-wide pieces. Stand potato pieces in large bowl of cold water for 30 minutes to avoid discolouration. Drain; pat dry with absorbent paper.
2 Heat oil in deep-fryer, wok or large saucepan; cook chips, in 3 batches, about 4 minutes each or until just tender but not browned. Drain on absorbent paper; stand 10 minutes.
3 Reheat oil; cook chips, in 3 batches, separating any that stick together by shaking deep-fryer basket or with a slotted spoon, until crisp and golden brown. Drain on absorbent paper.

SERVES 4
per serving 12g fat; 1015kJ (242 cal)

TIPS After the first cooking, the chips can stand for several hours before the final deep-frying.
Corn oil or vegetable oil can also be used.

Cut potatoes into 1cm slices, then cut each slice into 1cm-wide pieces

Drain the tender, but not browned, potato chips on absorbent paper

Chips should be golden brown in colour after the second frying

potato baskets with combination stir-fry

PREPARATION TIME 10 MINUTES (PLUS STANDING TIME) **COOKING TIME** 30 MINUTES

A wire potato basket, easily obtained from most Chinese supermarkets or catering supply stores, is in fact two metal baskets, one of which is small enough to fit inside the other, held together as a single tool by a clamp on the end of a long handle. You can also use bintje or russet burbank potatoes for this recipe.

1kg spunta potatoes, peeled
¼ cup (35g) cornflour
vegetable oil, for deep-frying

1 Using sharp knife, mandoline or V-slicer, cut potatoes into 2mm slices; cut each slice into 2mm-wide pieces. Toss potato pieces in large bowl with cornflour to coat.
2 Heat oil in deep-fryer, wok or large saucepan. Using fingers, line the larger of the baskets with a sixth of the potato mixture; clamp smaller basket down inside larger basket to secure potato mixture. Submerge basket in hot oil; deep-fry about 3 minutes or until browned lightly.
3 Unclamp the two wire baskets; gently remove potato basket by tapping on bench. Using metal tongs, carefully return potato basket to same hot oil about 2 minutes or until browned and crisp. Repeat basket-making with remaining potato mixture; fill baskets with combination stir-fry (see right).

MAKES 6
per basket 8.3g fat; 780kJ (186 cal)
per basket with stir-fry 28.6g fat; 2513kJ (600 cal)

TIP Baskets can be deep-fried up to 4 hours ahead. Cover and keep airtight when cool, then reheat by immersing briefly in hot oil until heated through.

Cut potatoes into 2mm slices, then cut each slice into 2mm-wide pieces

Using fingers, line larger of the baskets with a sixth of the potato mixture

Clamp smaller basket down inside larger basket to secure potato mixture

combination stir-fry

PREPARATION TIME 25 MINUTES (PLUS REFRIGERATION TIME) **COOKING TIME** 20 MINUTES

½ teaspoon salt
½ teaspoon bicarbonate of soda
1 tablespoon water
500g chicken breast fillets, sliced thinly
500g beef rump steak, sliced thinly
12 uncooked medium prawns (300g)
vegetable oil, for deep-frying
1 medium brown onion (150g), sliced thickly
1 medium carrot (120g), sliced thinly
1 small red capsicum (150g), sliced thinly
2 cups (170g) broccoli florets
100g mushrooms, quartered
100g snow peas, halved lengthways
100g baby corn, halved lengthways
2 cloves garlic, crushed
1 teaspoon grated fresh ginger
2 teaspoons cornflour
½ cup (125ml) chicken stock
⅓ cup (80ml) oyster sauce

1 Blend salt, soda and the water in medium bowl; add chicken and beef, stir to combine. Cover; refrigerate 1 hour.
2 Meanwhile, shell and devein prawns, leaving tails intact.
3 Heat oil in wok or large saucepan; deep-fry beef and chicken, in batches, until just cooked through. Drain on absorbent paper.
4 Reheat oil; deep-fry prawns and vegetables, in batches, until just tender. Drain on absorbent paper. Remove oil from wok; when cool, strain and reserve for future deep-frying.
5 Reheat wok; cook garlic and ginger, stirring, until fragrant. Return chicken, beef, prawns and vegetables to wok; stir-fry to combine. Add blended cornflour and stock, then sauce; stir-fry until sauce boils and thickens slightly.

TIP Keep the oil used for deep-frying for another time. After it has cooled completely, strain the oil through an absorbent-paper-lined sieve into a glass jar having a tight-fitting lid. Seal and store in the refrigerator until required. Depending on what has been deep-fried in the oil, it's possible to re-use it, as a deep-frying medium only, as many as three or four more times; when it starts to cloud or darken, discard it with other waste – not down the kitchen-sink drain.

potato skins

PREPARATION TIME 5 MINUTES (PLUS COOLING TIME) **COOKING TIME** 1 HOUR 10 MINUTES

Serve potato skins as dippers at your next cocktail party or as a great snack for the kids to nibble. You can also use desiree or pontiac potatoes for this recipe.

1kg russet burbank
   potatoes, unpeeled
2 tablespoons olive oil

1 Preheat oven to hot.
2 Scrub potatoes well; brush with half of the olive oil. Place potatoes on oven tray; bake, uncovered, in hot oven about 50 minutes or until tender. Cool.
3 Cut each potato into six wedges; carefully remove flesh, leaving skins intact. Place potato skins, skin-side down, on wire rack over oven tray; brush with remaining oil. Roast, uncovered, in hot oven about 20 minutes or until crisp; serve with any of the dips below.

SERVES 4
per serving 9.8g fat; 1034kJ (247 cal)

horseradish and sour cream
Combine 1 finely chopped small brown onion, ¼ cup horseradish cream, ¾ cup light sour cream, ¼ teaspoon sweet paprika and ¼ cup cream in small bowl.

MAKES 1½ CUPS
per tablespoon 3.6g fat; 161kJ (39 cal)

hummus
Blend or process 300g can rinsed drained chickpeas, 2 tablespoons lemon juice, 1 crushed garlic clove, ¼ cup olive oil, 2 tablespoons tahini and 2 tablespoons water until almost smooth.

MAKES 1¼ CUPS
per tablespoon 4.5g fat; 211kJ (51 cal)

olive tapenade
Blend or process 2 tablespoons toasted pine nuts, 2 cups seeded kalamata olives, 1 crushed garlic clove, 1 tablespoon lemon juice, 1 drained anchovy fillet and ¼ cup olive oil until almost smooth.

MAKES 1½ CUPS
per tablespoon 4.5g fat; 226kJ (54 cal)

Carefully scoop out the flesh from the wedges, leaving the skins intact

Place the potato skins on a wire rack over an oven tray, then brush with oil

Hot, crisp potato skins are delicious with the savoury dip of your choice

potato wedges

PREPARATION TIME 10 MINUTES **COOKING TIME** 40 MINUTES

The spice combinations below can be tossed with the oil and potato wedges before roasting, if desired. You can also use coliban or sebago potatoes for this recipe.

1kg kipfler potatoes, unpeeled
2 tablespoons olive oil

1 Preheat oven to moderately hot. Lightly oil two oven trays.
2 Cut each potato into wedges; toss potato wedges and oil in large bowl. Place wedges, in single layer, on prepared trays; roast, uncovered, turning occasionally, in moderately hot oven about 40 minutes or until crisp and cooked through.

SERVES 4
per serving 9.8g fat; 1034kJ (247 cal)
For a lower-fat version, use 1 lightly beaten egg white instead of olive oil.
per serving 0.3g fat; 698kJ (167 cal)

lemon pepper
Combine 1 tablespoon finely grated lemon rind, 1 tablespoon lemon juice and ½ teaspoon freshly ground black pepper in small bowl.

per serving (including wedges)
9.8g fat; 1046kJ (250 cal)

cajun
Combine ½ teaspoon ground oregano, 2 teaspoons ground cumin, 1 teaspoon hot paprika, ½ teaspoon ground black pepper, 1 teaspoon ground turmeric, 1 teaspoon ground coriander and ¼ teaspoon chilli powder in small bowl.

per serving (including wedges)
10.3g fat; 1082kJ (259 cal)

sun-dried tomato
Combine 1 tablespoon sun-dried tomato pesto, 2 teaspoons tomato sauce and 1 teaspoon sambal oelek in small bowl.

per serving (including wedges)
10.7g fat; 1093kJ (261 cal)

Kipfler potatoes must be scrubbed
well before being cut into wedges

Wedges can be coated in egg white
rather than oil for a lower-fat version

Bake the wedges, in a single layer,
on lightly greased oven trays

potato scallops

PREPARATION TIME 20 MINUTES (PLUS STANDING TIME) **COOKING TIME** 15 MINUTES

The potato scallop is an Australian favourite, delicious either on its own or used as a feature in a recipe, as we have done opposite. You can also use purple congo or spunta potatoes for this recipe.

500g russet burbank potatoes, peeled
1 tablespoon plain flour
¾ cup (110g) self-raising flour
1 cup (250ml) water
vegetable oil, for deep-frying

1 Using sharp knife, mandoline or V-slicer, cut potatoes into 2mm slices. Stand potato slices in large bowl of cold water for 30 minutes to avoid discolouration. Drain; pat dry with absorbent paper.
2 Meanwhile, place flours in medium bowl; add the water, whisk until batter is smooth.
3 Heat oil in wok or large saucepan. Dip potato slices, one at a time, in batter; deep-fry potato slices, in batches, until browned lightly and tender. Drain on absorbent paper. Serve scallops on their own or with smoked trout, as seen opposite.

MAKES 50
per scallop 0.9g fat; 90kJ (22 cal)

TIP You can use a beer batter for these scallops: simply substitute the water with 1 cup of beer.

Use the thin slicing insert of a V-slicer to cut the potatoes into 2mm slices

Using absorbent paper, pat the potato slices completely dry

Dip the potato slices, one at a time, in the batter before deep-frying

smoked trout and potato scallop stacks

PREPARATION TIME 15 MINUTES

½ cup (120g) sour cream
1 tablespoon lemon juice
1 tablespoon drained baby capers
12 cooked potato scallops
50g mesclun
1½ cups (260g) flaked
    smoked trout
1 small red onion (100g),
    sliced thinly

1 Combine sour cream, juice and capers in small bowl.
2 Place two potato scallops on each serving plate; top with a little of the mesclun, trout, onion and sour cream mixture. Place a third potato scallop on top of the stack, then garnish with more of the mesclun, trout, onion and sour cream mixture. Top with extra capers, if desired.

SERVES 4
per serving 15.2g fat; 906kJ (217 cal)

sautéed potatoes

PREPARATION TIME 5 MINUTES **COOKING TIME** 20 MINUTES

Sautéed potatoes are quick and easy to make. You can also use ghee, unsalted butter or a mixture of butter and oil, if you prefer, because all can be used over high heat without burning. You can also use bintje or russet burbank potatoes for this recipe.

1kg desiree potatoes, unpeeled
2 tablespoons olive oil
50g butter, chopped

1 Cut potatoes into 1cm slices.
2 Heat oil and butter in large non-stick frying pan; cook potato, covered, over medium heat, turning occasionally, until browned lightly. Reduce heat; cook, tossing pan to turn potato slices, about 10 minutes or until tender.

SERVES 4
per serving 20g fat; 1415kJ (338 cal)

Using a sharp knife, cut the unpeeled potatoes into 1cm slices

Melt the chopped butter with the oil in a large non-stick frying pan

Toss the potato slices in the frying pan until they are cooked through

straw potatoes

PREPARATION TIME 10 MINUTES (PLUS STANDING TIME) **COOKING TIME** 5 MINUTES

Straw potatoes, as their name implies, are meant to be as thin and crisp as a strand of farmyard straw. You can also use bintje or spunta potatoes for this recipe.

1kg russet burbank potatoes, peeled
peanut oil, for deep-frying

1 Using sharp knife, mandoline or V-slicer, cut potatoes into 2mm slices; cut each slice into 2mm-wide pieces. Stand potato pieces in large bowl of cold water for 30 minutes to avoid discolouration. Drain; pat dry with absorbent paper.
2 Heat oil in wok or large saucepan; deep-fry potato, in batches, until browned lightly. Drain on absorbent paper. Serve hot or cold, sprinkled with sea salt, if desired.

SERVES 6
per serving 9.3g fat; 726kJ (173 cal)

TIP Corn or vegetable oil can be used instead of the peanut oil.

potato and parsley wafers

PREPARATION TIME 30 MINUTES **COOKING TIME** 5 MINUTES

These wafers not only look fantastic, but they taste even better. You can also use russet burbank or spunta potatoes for this recipe.

500g bintje potatoes, peeled
1 bunch fresh flat-leaf parsley
vegetable oil, for deep-frying

1 Using sharp knife, mandoline or V-slicer, cut potatoes into 2mm slices.
2 Top half of the potato slices with parsley leaves; top with remaining potato slices, press firmly to seal wafers.
3 Heat oil in wok or large saucepan; deep-fry wafers, in batches, until browned lightly and crisp. Drain on absorbent paper.

SERVES 4
per serving 6.8g fat; 548kJ (131 cal)

TIP Try layering various herb leaves, such as sage, inside the potato wafers.

deep-fried crisps

PREPARATION TIME 10 MINUTES (PLUS STANDING TIME) **COOKING TIME** 20 MINUTES

After experiencing the flavour and crunchiness of homemade crisps, you will never need to open another packet again. You can also use russet burbank or spunta potatoes for this recipe.

1kg bintje potatoes, peeled
vegetable oil, for deep-frying

seasoned salt
½ teaspoon sweet paprika
1 teaspoon sea salt flakes
½ teaspoon freshly ground black pepper
pinch cayenne pepper

1 Using sharp knife, mandoline or V-slicer, cut potatoes into 2mm slices. Stand potato pieces in large bowl of cold water for 30 minutes to avoid discolouration. Drain; pat dry with absorbent paper.
2 Meanwhile, make seasoned salt.
3 Heat oil in wok or large saucepan; deep-fry potato, in batches, turning occasionally with slotted spoon, until browned lightly. Drain potato, in single layer, on absorbent paper; sprinkle with seasoned salt.
   seasoned salt Combine ingredients in small bowl.

SERVES 8
per serving 6g fat; 511kJ (122 cal)

tempura salt and pepper potatoes with mirin dressing

PREPARATION TIME 30 MINUTES (PLUS STANDING TIME) **COOKING TIME** 1 HOUR

Contrary to popular belief, tempura did not originate in Japan but was brought to the Land of the Rising Sun by Portuguese missionaries. You can also use purple congo or russet burbank potatoes for this recipe.

1 cup (150g) rice flour
1¾ cups (255g) cornflour
1¼ cups (310ml) chilled soda water
500g bintje potatoes, peeled
vegetable oil, for deep-frying

roasted salt and pepper spice
1 teaspoon sichuan peppercorns
1 tablespoon sea salt flakes
2 cinnamon sticks
4 star anise

mirin dressing
1 clove garlic, crushed
1 tablespoon finely chopped
   fresh ginger
¼ cup (60ml) soy sauce
2 fresh small red thai chillies,
   sliced thinly
½ cup (125ml) water
¼ cup (55g) sugar
¼ cup (60ml) mirin
1½ tablespoons rice wine vinegar

1 Place rice flour and 1 cup of the cornflour in medium bowl; add soda water, stir until just combined (batter should be lumpy). Cover; stand 30 minutes.
2 Using sharp knife, mandoline or V-slicer, cut potatoes into 2mm slices; dry with absorbent paper.
3 Make roasted salt and pepper spice and mirin dressing.
4 Heat oil in wok or large saucepan. Dust potato slices, one at a time, with remaining cornflour, then dip in batter; deep-fry potato, in batches, until browned lightly and tender. Drain on absorbent paper; sprinkle with roasted salt and pepper spice, serve with mirin dressing.
   roasted salt and pepper spice Preheat oven to slow. Sprinkle spices evenly onto oven tray; roast in slow oven 1 hour. Using mortar and pestle, or spice grinder, crush spices until powdered; push spice mixture through fine sieve into small bowl.
   mirin dressing Place ingredients in small saucepan; bring to a boil. Reduce heat; simmer, uncovered, 5 minutes.

SERVES 4
per serving 16.9g fat; 2771kJ (662 cal)

cottage fries

PREPARATION TIME 10 MINUTES (PLUS STANDING TIME) **COOKING TIME** 10 MINUTES

Also known as home-fried potatoes, cottage fries are thinly sliced potatoes that can be fried with either onion or green capsicum. You can also use bintje or spunta potatoes for this recipe.

1kg russet burbank potatoes, peeled
30g butter, chopped
½ cup (125ml) vegetable oil
1 medium brown onion (150g), sliced thickly

1 Using sharp knife, mandoline or V-slicer, slice potatoes into 2mm slices. Stand potato slices in large bowl of cold water for 30 minutes to avoid discolouration. Drain; pat dry with absorbent paper.
2 Heat a third of the butter and a third of the oil in large frying pan; cook a third of the potato and a third of the onion, stirring occasionally, until browned lightly and cooked through. Drain on absorbent paper; cover to keep warm. Repeat, making two more batches, with remaining butter, oil, potato and onion. Return cottage fries to pan; toss to combine, season with freshly cracked black pepper and sea salt, if desired.

SERVES 4
per serving 35.1g fat; 1911kJ (456 cal)

lyonnaise potatoes

PREPARATION TIME 10 MINUTES **COOKING TIME** 20 MINUTES

Lyon is seen as one of the gastronomic capitals of the world, and it's no wonder when the city produces luscious dishes such as this. You can also use desiree or ruby lou potatoes for this recipe.

900g desiree potatoes, peeled, chopped coarsely
1 tablespoon olive oil
2 medium red onions (340g), sliced thinly
3 cloves garlic, crushed
6 bacon rashers (420g), rind removed, chopped coarsely
¼ cup coarsely chopped fresh mint

1 Boil, steam or microwave potato until just tender; drain.
2 Meanwhile, heat half of the oil in large frying pan; cook onion and garlic, stirring, until onion softens. Remove from pan.
3 Cook bacon in same pan, stirring, until crisp; drain on absorbent paper.
4 Heat remaining oil in same pan; cook potato, stirring, about 5 minutes or until browned lightly.
5 Return onion mixture and bacon to pan; stir gently to combine with potato. Remove from heat; stir in mint.

SERVES 4
per serving 12.5g fat; 1253kJ (299 cal)

gremolata chips

PREPARATION TIME 20 MINUTES (PLUS REFRIGERATION TIME) **COOKING TIME** 15 MINUTES

Gremolata, a mixture of parsley, garlic and lemon rind, is usually sprinkled over slow-cooked meats, such as osso buco. It's wonderful for adding a refreshing flavour to dishes. You can also use desiree or pink fir apple potatoes for this recipe.

1 cup (70g) stale breadcrumbs
½ cup finely chopped fresh flat-leaf parsley
½ cup (80g) pine nuts, toasted, chopped finely
2 cloves garlic, crushed
2 tablespoons finely grated parmesan cheese
1 tablespoon finely grated lemon rind
3 medium king edward potatoes (500g), peeled
¼ cup (35g) plain flour
1 egg
2 tablespoons milk
2 tablespoons drained capers, rinsed
vegetable oil, for deep-frying
¼ cup (60g) sour cream
100g semi-dried tomatoes

1 Place breadcrumbs, parsley, nuts, garlic, cheese and rind in medium bowl; stir to combine.
2 Cut potatoes lengthways into four slices. Boil, steam or microwave potato until just tender; drain. Cool.
3 Coat each potato slice in flour; shake off excess. Dip each slice in combined egg and milk; toss in breadcrumb mixture, press to coat top and bottom of potato slices. Place on tray, cover; refrigerate 1 hour.
4 Meanwhile, dry capers on absorbent paper. Heat oil in wok or large saucepan; deep-fry capers until crisp. Remove with slotted spoon; drain on absorbent paper.
5 Reheat oil; deep-fry potato slices, in batches, until browned and crisp. Drain on absorbent paper.
6 Serve gremolata chips hot, topped with sour cream, semi-dried tomatoes and fried capers.

MAKES 12
per chip 12.1g fat; 785kJ (187 cal)

chicken and wedges salad

PREPARATION TIME 15 MINUTES **COOKING TIME** 40 MINUTES

You need to buy a large barbecued chicken weighing about a kilogram for this recipe; discard skin and bones, chop the meat coarsely. You can also use pontiac or sebago potatoes for this recipe.

750g king edward
   potatoes, unpeeled
1 tablespoon olive oil
4 bacon rashers (280g), rind
   removed, chopped coarsely
250g cherry tomatoes, halved
2 small lebanese cucumbers
   (260g), seeded, sliced thinly
1 small baby cos lettuce,
   leaves separated
2½ cups (425g) coarsely chopped
   cooked chicken

herb dressing
1 tablespoon white vinegar
1 tablespoon lemon juice
1 clove garlic, crushed
⅓ cup (80ml) olive oil
2 teaspoons finely chopped
   fresh basil
2 teaspoons finely chopped
   fresh oregano

1 Preheat oven to moderately hot. Lightly oil oven tray.
2 Cut each potato into six wedges; toss wedges in large bowl with oil. Place wedges, in single layer, on prepared tray; roast, uncovered, in moderately hot oven about 40 minutes or until browned lightly and tender.
3 Meanwhile, cook bacon in large heated non-stick frying pan, stirring, until crisp. Drain on absorbent paper.
4 Make herb dressing.
5 Combine wedges and bacon in large bowl with tomato, cucumber, lettuce and chicken. Add herb dressing; toss gently to combine.
   herb dressing Combine ingredients in screw-top jar; shake well.

SERVES 4
per serving 37.8g fat; 2626kJ (627 cal)

the perfect rösti

PREPARATION TIME 5 MINUTES **COOKING TIME** 20 MINUTES

Rösti, the classic Swiss potato cakes, are best made from a starchy potato, such as spunta or russet burbank, which is grated raw, then immediately cooked fairly slowly in butter. Perfect rösti have a thick crunchy crust and are moist and buttery inside.

1kg russet burbank potatoes, peeled
1 teaspoon salt
80g unsalted butter
2 tablespoons vegetable oil

1 Grate potatoes coarsely into large bowl; stir in salt, squeeze excess moisture from potatoes. Divide potato mixture into eight portions.
2 Heat 10g of the butter and 1 teaspoon of the oil in medium non-stick frying pan; spread one portion of the potato mixture over base of pan, flatten with spatula to form a firm pancake. Cook, uncovered, over medium heat, until golden brown on underside; shake pan to loosen rösti, then invert onto large plate. Gently slide rösti back into pan; cook, uncovered, until other side is golden brown and potato centre is tender. Drain on absorbent paper; cover to keep warm. Repeat with the same amounts of remaining butter, oil and potato mixture.

MAKES 8
per rösti 13g fat; 770kJ (184 cal)
For a lower-fat version, use low-fat dairy-free spread instead of the butter.
per rösti 8.7g fat; 606kJ (145 cal)

TIPS Rösti are best served immediately but can be kept, loosely covered with foil, in a slow oven for up to an hour.
Do not grate the potato until ready to cook rösti to avoid discolouring.

Use the largest holes of a four-sided grater to grate the potatoes coarsely

Flatten the potato mixture with a spatula to form a firm pancake

Invert the rösti onto a large plate, then gently slide it back into the pan

croquettes

pesto and mozzarella
croquettes

croquettes

PREPARATION TIME 20 MINUTES (PLUS REFRIGERATION TIME) **COOKING TIME** 25 MINUTES

1kg coliban potatoes, peeled,
   chopped coarsely
2 egg yolks
20g butter
½ cup (75g) plain flour
½ cup (60g) finely grated
   cheddar cheese
⅓ cup (50g) plain flour, extra
2 eggs
2 tablespoons milk
1 cup (100g) packaged
   breadcrumbs
vegetable oil, for deep-frying

1 Boil, steam or microwave potato until tender; drain. Mash potato in large bowl with yolks, butter, flour and cheese. Cover, refrigerate 30 minutes.
2 Using floured hands, shape heaped tablespoons of the potato mixture into fairly flat fish-finger shapes, dust with extra flour; shake away excess. Dip croquettes, one at a time, in combined eggs and milk, then in breadcrumbs. Refrigerate 30 minutes.
3 Heat oil in wok or large saucepan; deep-fry croquettes, in batches, until browned lightly. Drain on absorbent paper.

MAKES 24
per croquette 5.8g fat; 468kJ (112 cal)
For a lower-fat version, use low-fat dairy-free spread instead of the butter, reduced-fat cheddar cheese and no-fat milk.
per croquette 5.2g fat; 445kJ (106 cal)

TIP For a great variation, make pesto and mozzarella croquettes by blending or processing ¾ cup firmly packed fresh basil leaves, 1 tablespoon toasted pine nuts, 1 tablespoon finely grated parmesan cheese, 1 quartered garlic clove, 2 teaspoons lemon juice and 1 tablespoon olive oil, until almost smooth. Add pesto to croquette mixture. Mould croquettes into balls around 5mm-square pieces of mozzarella. **MAKES 32**
per croquette 5.8g fat; 408kJ (97 cal)

Croquettes can be shaped into fairly flat fish-finger shapes

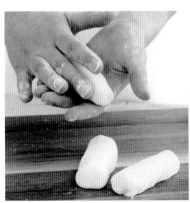
The most typical croquette is cylindrical in shape and fairly plump

Croquettes can also be shaped into balls and stuffed with a savoury filling

perfect salmon patties

PREPARATION TIME 20 MINUTES (PLUS REFRIGERATION TIME) **COOKING TIME** 20 MINUTES

Salmon patties are quite easy to make as all the necessary ingredients can usually be found in your pantry. You can also use coliban or nicola potatoes for this recipe.

1kg lasoda potatoes, peeled
440g can red salmon
1 small brown onion (80g), chopped finely
1 tablespoon finely chopped fresh flat-leaf parsley
1 teaspoon finely grated lemon rind
1 tablespoon lemon juice
½ cup (75g) plain flour
1 egg
2 tablespoons milk
½ cup (50g) packaged breadcrumbs
½ cup (35g) stale breadcrumbs
vegetable oil, for deep-frying

1 Boil, steam or microwave potatoes until tender; drain. Mash potato in large bowl.
2 Drain salmon; discard any skin and bones. Add salmon to potato with onion, parsley, rind and juice; mix well. Cover; refrigerate 30 minutes.
3 Using floured hands, shape salmon mixture into eight patties. Toss patties in flour; shake away excess. Dip patties, one at a time, in combined egg and milk, then in combined breadcrumbs.
4 Heat oil in wok or large saucepan; deep-fry patties, in batches, until browned lightly. Drain on absorbent paper.

MAKES 8
per patty 17.6g fat; 1415kJ (338 cal)

TIP Patties can be prepared a day ahead and refrigerated, covered.

Drain the salmon, then remove and discard any flakes of skin or bone

Using floured hands, shape the salmon mixture into eight patties

Dip the patties in combined egg and milk, then in combined breadcrumbs

potato cakes

PREPARATION TIME 15 MINUTES **COOKING TIME** 30 MINUTES

The combination of mashed potato, bacon, onion, cheese and sour cream in these cakes is so good you'll find it hard to stop at one. You can also use lasoda or pink-eye potatoes for this recipe.

1kg sebago potatoes, peeled, chopped coarsely
4 green onions, sliced thinly
4 bacon rashers (280g), rind removed, chopped finely
⅓ cup (40g) coarsely grated cheddar cheese
2 tablespoons sour cream
½ cup (75g) plain flour
50g butter
2 tablespoons olive oil

1 Boil, steam or microwave potato until tender; drain. Mash potato in large bowl until smooth.
2 Meanwhile, cook onion and bacon in small non-stick frying pan, stirring, until bacon is crisp. Add bacon mixture to potato with cheese and sour cream; stir to combine.
3 Using floured hands, shape potato mixture into 12 patties; roll in flour, shake off excess.
4 Heat butter and oil in large frying pan; cook potato cakes, in batches, until browned lightly both sides. Serve with lemon wedges, if desired.

MAKES 12
per cake 10.8g fat; 743kJ (178 cal)
For a lower-fat version, use reduced-fat cheddar cheese and light sour cream.
per cake 9.8g fat; 710kJ (170 cal)

hash browns

PREPARATION TIME 10 MINUTES (PLUS COOLING TIME) **COOKING TIME** 30 MINUTES

Originally called "hashed brown potatoes", this popular American dish can be eaten at breakfast, lunch or dinner. Ghee is butter that has been clarified to remove the milk solids; this enables it to be heated to a high temperature without burning. You can also use bintje or desiree potatoes for this recipe.

1kg sebago potatoes, unpeeled
1 small brown onion (80g),
   chopped finely
2 teaspoons finely chopped
   fresh rosemary
60g ghee

1 Boil, steam or microwave potatoes until just tender; drain. Cool 10 minutes.
2 Peel potatoes, cut into 1cm cubes. Combine potato in large bowl with onion and rosemary.
3 Heat a third of the ghee in medium heavy-based frying pan; place four egg rings in pan. Spoon ¼ cup of the potato mixture into each egg ring; using spatula, spread mixture evenly to fill ring. Cook, pressing frequently with spatula, until browned; carefully turn each ring to brown other side. Drain on absorbent paper; cover to keep warm. Repeat with the same amounts of remaining ghee and potato mixture.

MAKES 12
per hash brown 5.1g fat; 385kJ (92 cal)

TIPS Chives, thyme or parsley can be used instead of the rosemary.
A mixture of half olive oil and half melted butter can be used instead of ghee.

sour cream and chive potato pancakes

PREPARATION TIME 20 MINUTES **COOKING TIME** 15 MINUTES

It is important to squeeze as much excess moisture as possible from the potato so that the pancakes hold their shape while cooking. You can also use russet burbank or spunta potatoes for this recipe.

900g sebago potatoes, peeled
1 medium brown onion (150g),
    chopped finely
¼ cup finely chopped fresh chives
2 eggs, separated
2 tablespoons plain flour
½ cup (120g) sour cream
⅔ cup (160ml) vegetable oil
80g butter

1 Grate potatoes coarsely; squeeze excess moisture from potato with hands. Combine potato in large bowl with onion, chives, egg yolks, flour and sour cream.

2 Beat egg whites in small bowl with electric mixer until firm peaks form; gently fold into potato mixture.

3 Heat 2 tablespoons of the oil with 20g of the butter in large non-stick frying pan; cook heaped tablespoons of the potato mixture, uncovered, until browned both sides. Drain on absorbent paper; cover to keep warm. Repeat with the same amounts of remaining oil, butter and potato mixture.

MAKES 20
per pancake 13.6g fat; 642kJ (153 cal)

chorizo and potato fritters

PREPARATION TIME 25 MINUTES (PLUS COOLING TIME) **COOKING TIME** 15 MINUTES

You can also use russet burbank or spunta potatoes for this recipe.

2 teaspoons vegetable oil
1 chorizo sausage (200g), chopped finely
1 small brown onion (80g), chopped finely
2 fresh small red thai chillies, seeded, chopped finely
2 medium zucchini (240g), grated coarsely
450g bintje potatoes, peeled, grated coarsely
1 small kumara (250g), peeled, grated coarsely
3 eggs, beaten lightly
1 cup (150g) plain flour
1 teaspoon sweet paprika
vegetable oil, for deep-frying

sweet chilli dipping sauce
½ cup (120g) sour cream
2 tablespoons sweet chilli sauce

1 Heat oil in medium frying pan; cook chorizo, onion and chilli, stirring, until onion softens. Add zucchini; cook, stirring, 1 minute. Cool 10 minutes.
2 Meanwhile, make sweet chilli dipping sauce.
3 Combine chorizo mixture in large bowl with potato, kumara, eggs, flour and paprika.
4 Heat oil in wok or large saucepan; deep-fry level tablespoons of the potato mixture, in batches, until fritters are browned lightly. Drain on absorbent paper; serve with sweet chilli dipping sauce.
sweet chilli dipping sauce Combine ingredients in small bowl.

MAKES 40
per fritter 4.1g fat; 269kJ (64 cal)
per tablespoon sauce 6g fat; 252kJ (60 cal)

smoked trout potato cakes

PREPARATION TIME 25 MINUTES **COOKING TIME** 45 MINUTES

You can also use nicola or pink-eye potatoes for this recipe.

1kg sebago potatoes, peeled,
   chopped coarsely
1 clove garlic, crushed
¼ cup (35g) plain flour
2 eggs, beaten lightly
½ cup coarsely chopped
   fresh coriander
1 teaspoon sambal oelek
1 teaspoon finely grated
   lime rind
1 tablespoon lime juice
2 whole smoked trout (390g),
   skinned, boned,
   flaked coarsely

1 Preheat oven to moderate.
   Lightly oil two oven trays.
2 Boil, steam or microwave potato
   until tender; drain. Mash potato
   in large bowl. Add garlic, flour,
   eggs, coriander, sambal, rind
   and juice; stir to combine.
   Fold in trout.
3 Using floured hands, shape
   potato mixture into 12 patties;
   place patties on prepared trays.
   Bake, uncovered, in moderate
   oven about 30 minutes or until
   potato cakes are browned lightly.
   Serve with lime wedges and
   sweet chilli sauce, if desired.

MAKES 12
per cake 1.9g fat; 396kJ (95 cal)

prosciutto and roast capsicum rösti stacks

PREPARATION TIME 15 MINUTES **COOKING TIME** 30 MINUTES

Prosciutto – cured, air-dried ham – is usually sold thinly sliced at your local delicatessen. You can also use spunta or purple congo potatoes for this recipe.

1 small red capsicum (150g)
1 small yellow capsicum (150g)
⅓ cup (90g) tomato relish
1kg russet burbank
   potatoes, peeled
80g unsalted butter
2 teaspoons olive oil
8 slices prosciutto (120g)
20g baby spinach leaves
50g parmesan cheese, shaved

1 Quarter capsicums; remove and discard seeds and membranes. Roast capsicum under grill or in very hot oven, skin-side up, until skin blisters and blackens. Cover capsicum with plastic or paper 5 minutes. Peel away skin; slice capsicum thinly. Combine capsicum and relish in small bowl.

2 Meanwhile, grate potatoes coarsely; squeeze excess moisture from potato with hands, transfer to large bowl. Divide into eight portions.

3 Heat 10g of the butter in 20cm non-stick frying pan; spread one portion of the potato mixture over base of pan, flatten with spatula to form a firm pancake. Cook, uncovered, over medium heat, until golden brown on underside; shake pan to loosen rösti, then invert onto large plate. Gently slide rösti back into pan; cook, uncovered, until other side is golden brown and potato centre is tender. Drain on absorbent paper; cover to keep warm. Repeat with the same amounts of remaining butter and potato mixture.

4 Heat oil in same frying pan; cook prosciutto until crisp. Place one rösti on each of four serving plates, top with spinach, prosciutto, capsicum mixture and cheese, then with a second rösti.

SERVES 4
per serving 29.4g fat; 1972kJ (471 cal)
For a lower-fat version, use low-fat dairy-free spread instead of the butter.
per serving 18.4g fat; 1562kJ (373 cal)

creamed-corn and potato patties

PREPARATION TIME 25 MINUTES **COOKING TIME** 30 MINUTES

800g sebago potatoes, peeled
1 corn cob, husk and
　silk removed
2 egg yolks
310g can creamed corn
¾ cup (45g) fresh breadcrumbs
¼ cup finely chopped fresh
　flat-leaf parsley
¼ cup (35g) plain flour
50g butter
¼ cup (60ml) vegetable oil

1 Boil, steam or microwave potatoes until tender; drain.
2 Meanwhile, using sharp knife, remove kernels from corn cob.
3 Mash potatoes in large bowl until smooth. Add corn kernels, yolks, creamed corn, breadcrumbs and parsley; stir to combine.
4 Using floured hands, shape mixture into 12 patties. Toss patties in flour, shake away excess. Heat a third of the butter and 1 tablespoon of the oil in large frying pan; cook four patties, uncovered, until browned both sides. Repeat with the same amounts of remaining butter, oil and patties. Serve with crispy bacon, if desired.

MAKES 12
per patty 9.6g fat;
763kJ (182 cal)
For a lower-fat version, use low-fat dairy-free spread instead of the butter.
per patty 7.8g fat;
697kJ (167 cal)

mediterranean potato pancakes

PREPARATION TIME 30 MINUTES (PLUS COOLING AND REFRIGERATION TIMES) **COOKING TIME** 45 MINUTES

You can also use coliban or sebago potatoes for this recipe.

1 tablespoon olive oil
1 medium red onion (170g),
    chopped coarsely
2 cloves garlic, crushed
1 medium red capsicum (200g),
    chopped coarsely
1 medium yellow capsicum (200g),
    chopped coarsely
250g mushrooms,
    chopped coarsely
¼ cup (60ml) dry red wine
2 medium egg tomatoes (150g),
    chopped coarsely
2 x 425g cans crushed tomatoes
200g russet burbank potatoes,
    peeled, chopped coarsely
¾ cup (110g) plain flour
¼ teaspoon bicarbonate of soda
2 eggs
1¾ cups (430ml) buttermilk
½ cup coarsely chopped fresh basil
½ cup (40g) coarsely grated
    parmesan cheese

1 Heat oil in large frying pan; cook onion and garlic, stirring, until onion softens. Add capsicums and mushroom; cook, stirring, until vegetables are just tender. Add wine, fresh tomato and 1 can of the undrained tomatoes; bring to a boil. Reduce heat; simmer, uncovered, about 10 minutes or until mixture thickens slightly.

2 Meanwhile, boil, steam or microwave potato until tender; drain. Mash potato in large bowl; cool 10 minutes.

3 Mix combined sifted flour and soda with potato; gradually whisk in combined eggs and buttermilk until batter is smooth. Cover; refrigerate 10 minutes.

4 Preheat oven to moderate. Heat large lightly oiled frying pan; cook 4 x ¼-cups of the batter until browned lightly both sides. Repeat with the same amounts of remaining batter. Cool pancakes 10 minutes.

5 Divide vegetable mixture among pancakes; roll to enclose filling. Place pancakes, seam-side down, in shallow 3-litre (12-cup) baking dish.

6 Combine remaining can of undrained tomatoes and basil in small bowl; pour over pancakes, sprinkle with cheese. Bake, uncovered, in moderate oven about 15 minutes or until heated through.

MAKES 12
per pancake 6.5g fat; 642kJ (153 cal)

fetta and spinach stuffed potato balls

PREPARATION TIME 35 MINUTES **COOKING TIME** 30 MINUTES

You can also use lasoda or pink-eye potatoes for this recipe.

450g sebago potatoes, peeled, chopped coarsely
50g butter
⅔ cup (160ml) water
1 teaspoon salt
½ cup (75g) plain flour
2 eggs
vegetable oil, for deep-frying

spinach filling
180g spinach leaves, shredded finely
150g fetta, crumbled

1 Boil, steam or microwave potato until tender; drain. Mash in large bowl; cover to keep warm.
2 Meanwhile, make spinach filling.
3 Melt butter in medium saucepan, add the water and salt; bring to a boil. Remove from heat; immediately stir in flour. Using a wooden spoon, beat until mixture forms a smooth ball. Beat in eggs and potato, beating until smooth.
4 Roll level tablespoons of the dough into balls; use finger to press hole into centre of each ball. Fill holes with level teaspoons of the spinach filling; roll potato balls gently to enclose filling.
5 Heat oil in wok or large saucepan; deep-fry balls, in batches, until browned lightly. Drain on absorbent paper.
   spinach filling Boil, steam or microwave spinach until just wilted; drain. Rinse under cold water; drain. Squeeze as much excess liquid from spinach as possible. Combine spinach in medium bowl with cheese.

MAKES 24
per ball 6.2g fat; 351kJ (84 cal)

latkes

PREPARATION TIME 15 MINUTES   **COOKING TIME** 15 MINUTES

Latkes are fried potato pancakes traditionally eaten during Hanukkah because of the significance of oil in this Jewish festival. They're generally made from matzo meal but you can substitute polenta as we have here. You can also use russet burbank or spunta potatoes for this recipe.

1kg king edward potatoes, peeled
1 large brown onion (200g),
   chopped finely
2 eggs, beaten lightly
⅓ cup (55g) polenta
⅓ cup (80ml) vegetable oil
⅓ cup (100g) bottled apple sauce
2 tablespoons sour cream

1 Grate potatoes coarsely; squeeze excess moisture from potato with hands. Combine potato in large bowl with onion, eggs and polenta.
2 Using floured hands, shape potato mixture into 12 rounds.
3 Heat oil in large frying pan; cook latkes, in batches, until browned lightly both sides. Drain on absorbent paper; serve topped with apple sauce and sour cream.

MAKES 12
per latke 8.7g fat; 634kJ (152 cal)
For a lower-fat version, use light sour cream.
per latke 8.1g fat; 611kJ (146 cal)

potato blini with salsa cruda

PREPARATION TIME 30 MINUTES (PLUS STANDING TIME) **COOKING TIME** 30 MINUTES

You can also use nicola or sebago potatoes for this recipe.

200g russet burbank potatoes, peeled
¾ cup (110g) self-raising flour
½ teaspoon bicarbonate of soda
1 teaspoon finely grated lemon rind
¾ cup (180ml) milk
1 egg
100g butter, melted

salsa cruda
¼ cup (60ml) lemon juice
¼ cup (60ml) extra virgin olive oil
1 clove garlic, crushed
2 medium tomatoes (380g), seeded, chopped finely
½ cup finely chopped fresh flat-leaf parsley
1 small red onion (100g), chopped finely
1 small avocado (200g), chopped finely
1 tablespoon drained baby capers

horseradish topping
1 teaspoon horseradish cream
⅓ cup (80g) sour cream
¼ teaspoon sweet paprika

1 Boil, steam or microwave potatoes until tender; drain. Mash potatoes in large bowl. Stir in sifted flour and soda.
2 Make a well in the centre of potato mixture; pour in combined rind, milk and egg, stirring, until batter is smooth. Cover; stand 10 minutes.
3 Meanwhile, make salsa cruda and horseradish topping.
4 Heat large non-stick frying pan; brush lightly with a little of the butter. Cook tablespoons of the batter, in five batches, until browned both sides, brushing pan with butter between batches. Transfer to wire rack to cool. To serve, top blini with salsa cruda and horseradish topping.
salsa cruda Combine ingredients in medium bowl.
horseradish topping Combine ingredients in small bowl.

MAKES 25
per blini 8.7g fat; 433kJ (104 cal)
For a lower-fat version, use no-fat milk, low-fat dairy-free spread instead of the butter, and light sour cream.
per blini 6.1g fat; 341kJ (82 cal)

spicy potato pakoras with coriander raita

PREPARATION TIME 20 MINUTES (PLUS COOLING AND REFRIGERATION TIMES) **COOKING TIME** 20 MINUTES

Besan, a flour made from ground dried chickpeas, is a staple of the Indian kitchen and is used to make roti, chapati and other breads. Pakoras are small Indian fritters that can contain vegetables, meat, fish or rice. You can also use desiree potatoes for this recipe.

400g russet burbank potatoes, peeled,
   cut into 1cm cubes
1 small kumara (250g), peeled, cut into 1cm cubes
1½ cups (225g) besan
½ teaspoon bicarbonate of soda
¾ cup (180ml) water
2 teaspoons peanut oil
2 cloves garlic, crushed
½ teaspoon ground turmeric
1 teaspoon ground cumin
½ teaspoon dried chilli flakes
2 green onions, chopped finely
vegetable oil, for deep-frying

coriander raita
1 cup (280g) greek-style yogurt
½ cup coarsely chopped fresh coriander
1 teaspoon ground cumin

1. Boil, steam or microwave potato and kumara, together, until just tender; drain. Cool 10 minutes.
2. Meanwhile, make coriander raita.
3. Sift besan and soda into large bowl; gradually add the water, stirring, until batter is smooth.
4. Heat peanut oil in small frying pan; cook garlic, spices and chilli flakes, stirring, until fragrant. Combine garlic mixture in bowl with batter; stir in potato, kumara and onion.
5. Heat vegetable oil in wok or large saucepan; deep-fry tablespoons of the mixture, in batches, until pakoras are browned lightly. Drain on absorbent paper; serve with coriander raita.
   coriander raita Combine ingredients in small bowl. Cover; refrigerate 30 minutes.

MAKES 24
per pakora 3.4g fat; 302kJ (72 cal)
per tablespoon raita 1.4g fat; 100kJ (24 cal)

polenta and parmesan crusted fritters

PREPARATION TIME 20 MINUTES **COOKING TIME** 25 MINUTES

You can also use coliban or lasoda potatoes for this recipe.

1kg bintje potatoes, peeled
100g prosciutto, chopped finely
1 medium red onion (170g), sliced thinly
150g fennel, sliced thinly
1 egg, beaten lightly
⅓ cup (50g) plain flour
⅓ cup (55g) polenta
½ cup (40g) finely grated parmesan cheese
¼ cup (60ml) olive oil

1 Boil, steam or microwave potatoes until tender; drain. Mash potatoes in large bowl; stir in prosciutto, onion, fennel, egg and flour.
2 Using floured hands, shape potato mixture into eight patties; coat in combined polenta and cheese.
3 Heat oil in medium frying pan; cook patties, in batches, until fritters are browned both sides. Drain on absorbent paper.

MAKES 8
per fritter 10.5g fat; 970kJ (232 cal)

goat cheese and potato fritters

PREPARATION TIME 10 MINUTES **COOKING TIME** 20 MINUTES

You can also use pink-eye or sebago potatoes for this recipe.

600g pontiac potatoes, peeled
¼ cup (60ml) cream
¼ teaspoon ground nutmeg
3 eggs, beaten lightly
2 egg yolks, beaten lightly
½ cup (75g) plain flour
250g firm goat
    cheese, crumbled
2 tablespoons coarsely chopped
    fresh flat-leaf parsley
pinch cayenne pepper
vegetable oil, for deep-frying

1 Boil, steam or microwave potatoes until tender; drain. Mash potatoes in large bowl with cream and nutmeg until smooth. Add eggs and egg yolks; using wooden spoon, beat until smooth. Stir in flour, cheese, parsley and pepper.

2 Heat oil in wok or large saucepan; deep-fry level tablespoons of the potato mixture, in batches, until fritters are browned lightly. Drain on absorbent paper.

MAKES 32
per fritter 4.8g fat;
288kJ (69 cal)

the perfect roast potato

PREPARATION TIME 10 MINUTES (PLUS COOLING TIME) **COOKING TIME** 55 MINUTES

Perfectly roasted potatoes should be crisp and golden brown on the outside, and densely smooth and moist on the inside; full-flavoured and rich but never greasy. Olive oil is better to brush potatoes with than any other oil or butter because it tolerates high oven temperatures and lends its pleasant taste to the potatoes. Gently raking along the length of the peeled potato surface with the tines of a fork assists in crisping. Don't crowd potatoes on the oven tray because they will brown unevenly, and make certain the oven has reached the correct temperature before the tray goes in. Other varieties good for roasting are kipfler, lasoda and pink-eye.

6 pontiac potatoes (1.3kg), peeled, halved horizontally
2 tablespoons light olive oil

1 Preheat oven to hot. Lightly oil oven tray.
2 Boil, steam or microwave potatoes 5 minutes; drain. Pat dry with absorbent paper; cool 10 minutes.
3 Gently rake rounded sides of potatoes with tines of fork; place potatoes in single layer, cut-side down, on prepared oven tray. Brush with oil; roast, uncovered, in hot oven about 50 minutes or until potatoes are browned and crisp.

SERVES 4
per serving 9.8g fat; 1106kJ (264 cal)

Pat the potato halves dry with an absorbent paper towel

Gently rake the potato's surface with the tines of a fork to assist in crisping

Place potatoes in single layer on the oven tray before brushing with the oil

hasselback potatoes

PREPARATION TIME 20 MINUTES **COOKING TIME** 1 HOUR 10 MINUTES

This Swedish version of roasted potatoes produces a wonderfully crisp crust and makes an excellent accompaniment to roasts. You can also use ruby lou potatoes for this recipe.

6 desiree potatoes (1.1kg), peeled, halved horizontally
40g butter, melted
2 tablespoons olive oil
¼ cup (25g) packaged breadcrumbs
½ cup (60g) finely grated cheddar cheese

1 Preheat oven to moderate.
2 Place one potato half, cut-side down, on chopping board; place a chopstick on board along each side of potato. Slice potato thinly, cutting through to chopsticks to prevent cutting all the way through. Repeat with remaining potato halves.
3 Coat potato halves in combined butter and oil in medium baking dish; place, rounded-side up, in single layer. Roast, uncovered, in moderate oven 45 minutes, brushing frequently with oil mixture. Continue roasting without brushing about 15 minutes or until potatoes are cooked through.
4 Sprinkle combined breadcrumbs and cheese over potatoes; roast, uncovered, in moderate oven about 10 minutes or until topping is browned lightly.

SERVES 4
per serving 23.2g fat; 1641kJ (392 cal)
For a lower-fat version, use low-fat dairy-free spread instead of the butter, and reduced-fat cheddar cheese.
per serving 17.5g fat; 1434kJ (343 cal)

Place a chopstick on chopping board along each side of the potato half

Slice the potato to the chopsticks to prevent cutting all the way through

Sprinkle the combined cheese and breadcrumbs over potatoes

baked potatoes

PREPARATION TIME 5 MINUTES **COOKING TIME** 1 HOUR

The perfect baked potato should be salty and crisp on the outside and snow white and fluffy on the inside. You can also use russet burbank or spunta potatoes for this recipe.

8 king edward potatoes (1.4kg), unpeeled

1 Preheat oven to moderate.
2 Pierce skin of each potato with fork; wrap each potato in foil, place on oven tray. Bake in moderate oven about 1 hour or until tender. Top with one of the variations below.

MAKES 8
per potato 0.2g fat; 478kJ (114 cal)

Pierce the skin of each potato to avoid it splitting in the oven

Wrapping the potatoes completely in foil results in a soft skin after baking

A lightly oiled potato rolled in sea salt will result in a crisp crunchy skin

toppings

PREPARATION TIME 5 MINUTES

Each of these toppings is enough to top the eight potatoes above.

cream cheese and pesto

Combine ⅔ cup spreadable cream cheese, ½ teaspoon cracked black pepper and ⅓ cup pesto in small bowl; refrigerate until required.

per potato 10g fat; 911kJ (218 cal)

lime and chilli yogurt

Combine ⅔ cup yogurt, 2 tablespoons coarsely chopped fresh coriander, 2 fresh small seeded finely chopped red thai chillies and 1 teaspoon finely grated lime rind in small bowl; refrigerate until required.

per potato 1g fat; 551kJ (132 cal)

mustard and walnut butter

Mash 60g softened butter, 1 teaspoon wholegrain mustard and 2 tablespoons finely chopped toasted walnuts in small bowl until mixture forms a paste; refrigerate until required.

per potato 7.8g fat; 769kJ (184 cal)

lime and chilli yogurt

cream cheese and pesto

mustard and walnut butter

potatoes anna

PREPARATION TIME 20 MINUTES **COOKING TIME** 50 MINUTES

In the late 1800s, French chef Adolphe Duglére devised this dish in honour of Anna Deslions, a courtesan who entertained clients in a private dining room within his restaurant. You can also use coliban potatoes for this recipe.

1.2kg ruby lou potatoes, peeled
100g butter, melted

1 Preheat oven to very hot. Lightly oil shallow 26cm-round (2-litre) baking dish.
2 Using sharp knife, mandoline or V-slicer, cut potatoes into very thin slices; pat dry with absorbent paper.
3 Place a single layer of potato, slightly overlapping, in prepared dish; brush with a little of the butter. Continue layering remaining potato and butter, cover dish with foil; bake in very hot oven for 20 minutes.
4 Remove foil; use metal spatula to press down on potato. Reduce oven temperature to hot; bake, uncovered, about 30 minutes or until top is crisp and browned lightly. Cut into wedges to serve.

SERVES 6
per serving 13.8g fat; 972kJ (232 cal)
For a lower-fat version, use low-fat dairy-free spread instead of the butter.
per serving 6.8g fat; 707kJ (169 cal)

timbale brabant

PREPARATION TIME 25 MINUTES **COOKING TIME** 30 MINUTES (PLUS STANDING TIME)

This dish was introduced to the world by a Cajun cook in New Orleans, but we bet the idea – as well as the name – originally came from a French settler to Louisiana. No matter what the origin, the taste is pure heaven. You can also use desiree or pontiac potatoes for this recipe.

500g ruby lou
   potatoes, unpeeled
100g butter, melted
2 cloves garlic, crushed
¾ cup (60g) finely grated
   parmesan cheese
6 green onions, sliced thinly
½ cup coarsely chopped fresh
   flat-leaf parsley

1 Preheat oven to moderately hot. Line bases of four 1-cup (250ml) metal moulds with baking paper.
2 Using sharp knife, mandoline or V-slicer, cut potatoes into very thin slices; pat dry with absorbent paper. Place a few potato slices in each mould, sprinkle with a little combined butter and garlic, cheese, onion and parsley. Continue layering remaining ingredients, finishing with potato; cover each mould with foil, place on oven tray. Bake in moderately hot oven about 30 minutes or until potato is tender. Stand 5 minutes before turning out.

SERVES 4
per serving 25.6g fat; 1406kJ (336 cal)
For a lower-fat version, use low-fat dairy-free spread instead of the butter.
per serving 14.9g fat; 1008kJ (241 cal)

scalloped potatoes

PREPARATION TIME 20 MINUTES **COOKING TIME** 1 HOUR 10 MINUTES (PLUS STANDING TIME)

This scrumptious layered dish of potato, ham, cream and cheese is certain to become one of your family's favourites. You can also use coliban or sebago potatoes for this recipe.

1.2kg desiree potatoes, peeled
150g leg ham, chopped finely
300ml cream
¾ cup (180ml) milk
¾ cup (90g) coarsely grated
    cheddar cheese

1 Preheat oven to moderate; oil
   1.5-litre (6-cup) baking dish.
2 Using sharp knife, mandoline or
   V-slicer, cut potatoes into very thin
   slices; pat dry with absorbent
   paper. Layer a quarter of the
   potato in prepared dish; top with
   a third of the ham. Continue
   layering remaining potato and
   ham, finishing with potato.
3 Heat cream and milk in small
   saucepan until almost boiling;
   pour over potato mixture. Cover
   with foil; bake in moderate oven
   30 minutes. Remove foil; bake
   20 minutes. Top with cheese;
   bake, uncovered, about
   20 minutes or until potato
   is tender. Stand 10 minutes
   before serving.

SERVES 6
per serving 28.7g fat;
1745kJ (417 cal)

potatoes byron

PREPARATION TIME 10 MINUTES (PLUS COOLING TIME) **COOKING TIME** 1 HOUR 10 MINUTES

Mashed potato, cream and cheese, what else do you need? One spoonful of this delectable dish and the answer will most certainly be "nothing". You can also use pink-eye or sebago potatoes for this recipe.

1kg russet burbank
    potatoes, unpeeled
60g butter, chopped
½ cup (125ml) cream
¼ cup (20g) finely grated
    parmesan cheese
¼ cup (30g) finely grated
    gruyère cheese

1 Preheat oven to moderate; oil four shallow 1-cup (250ml) ovenproof dishes.
2 Pierce skin of each potato with fork; place on oven tray. Bake, uncovered, in moderate oven about 1 hour or until tender. Cover; cool 10 minutes. Increase oven temperature to hot.
3 Split potatoes in half lengthways; scoop flesh into medium bowl, discard potato skins. Mash potato with butter.
4 Centre a 7.5cm cutter in one prepared dish; pack mashed potato into cutter. Carefully remove cutter; repeat, packing remaining potato into cutter in each dish. Pour cream evenly over dishes; sprinkle with combined cheeses. Bake, uncovered, in moderate oven about 10 minutes or until heated through and browned lightly.

SERVES 4
per serving 29.8g fat; 1871kJ (447 cal)
For a lower-fat version, use low-fat dairy-free spread instead of the butter, and light cream.
per serving 16.7g fat; 1400kJ (334 cal)

portuguese potatoes

PREPARATION TIME 15 MINUTES COOKING TIME 50 MINUTES

Piri-piri is a hot Portuguese sauce made of chilli, garlic, ginger, oil and herbs, and is available from supermarkets. You can also use pontiac potatoes for this recipe.

600g sebago potatoes, peeled, chopped coarsely
2 tablespoons olive oil
2 cloves garlic, crushed
1 large brown onion (200g), chopped coarsely
4 medium tomatoes (760g), chopped coarsely
2 teaspoons sweet paprika
2 teaspoons finely chopped fresh thyme
½ cup (125ml) chicken stock
1 tablespoon piri-piri sauce
1 tablespoon coarsely chopped fresh flat-leaf parsley

1 Preheat oven to hot.
2 Toss potato and half of the oil in medium shallow baking dish. Roast, uncovered, in hot oven about 30 minutes or until browned lightly.
3 Meanwhile, heat remaining oil in large frying pan; cook garlic and onion, stirring, until onion softens. Add tomato, paprika and thyme; cook, stirring, about 1 minute or until tomato just softens. Add stock and sauce; bring to a boil. Reduce heat; simmer, uncovered, stirring occasionally, about 10 minutes or until sauce thickens slightly.
4 Remove potato from oven; reduce oven temperature to moderate.
5 Pour sauce over potato; bake, uncovered, in moderate oven about 20 minutes or until potato is tender. Serve sprinkled with parsley.

SERVES 6
per serving 6.7g fat; 604kJ (144 cal)

creamed potatoes with rosemary and cheese

PREPARATION TIME 15 MINUTES **COOKING TIME** 1 HOUR 20 MINUTES (PLUS STANDING TIME)

You can also use desiree or russet burbank potatoes for this recipe.

1kg spunta potatoes, peeled
300ml cream
2 cloves garlic, crushed
2 chicken stock cubes, crumbled
¼ teaspoon cracked black pepper
1 tablespoon finely chopped
    fresh rosemary
½ cup (40g) finely grated
    parmesan cheese

1 Preheat oven to moderate; oil shallow 2.5-litre (10-cup) ovenproof dish.
2 Using sharp knife, mandoline or V-slicer, cut potatoes into thin slices; pat dry with absorbent paper. Combine cream, garlic, stock cubes, pepper and rosemary in small bowl.
3 Layer a quarter of the potato slices, slightly overlapping, in prepared dish; top with a quarter of the cream mixture. Continue layering remaining potato and cream mixture.
4 Press potato firmly with spatula to completely submerge in cream, cover with foil; bake in moderate oven 1 hour. Remove foil; sprinkle with cheese. Bake, uncovered, about 20 minutes or until potato is tender and cheese browns lightly. Stand 10 minutes before serving.

SERVES 6
per serving 23.9g fat; 1359kJ (325 cal)
For a lower-fat version, use light cream.
per serving 13.2g fat; 987kJ (236 cal)

tiella

PREPARATION TIME 30 MINUTES (PLUS STANDING TIME) **COOKING TIME** 1 HOUR 30 MINUTES

From the Apulia region in the south-east of Italy, a tiella is both a homely recipe made with eggplant and potatoes, and the name of the dish in which it is traditionally cooked. You can also use desiree or spunta potatoes for this recipe.

2 small eggplants (460g)
2 tablespoons coarse
    cooking salt
1kg medium tomatoes, peeled,
    seeded, chopped finely
1 medium brown onion (150g),
    chopped finely
2 trimmed sticks celery (150g),
    chopped finely
2 cloves garlic, crushed
1 tablespoon finely chopped
    fresh oregano
1 tablespoon finely chopped
    fresh flat-leaf parsley
1kg sebago potatoes, peeled
¼ cup (60ml) olive oil
2 tablespoons fresh
    oregano leaves

1 Cut eggplants into thin slices, sprinkle with salt; stand in colander in sink or over large bowl 30 minutes. Rinse eggplant well under cold water; pat dry with absorbent paper.
2 Preheat oven to moderate.
3 Combine tomato, onion, celery, garlic, chopped oregano and parsley in medium bowl.
4 Using sharp knife, mandoline or V-slicer, cut potatoes into thin slices; pat dry with absorbent paper. Place half of the potato in lightly oiled shallow 2-litre (8-cup) baking dish; top with half of the eggplant, half of the tomato mixture, then drizzle with half of the oil. Repeat layering with remaining potato, eggplant, tomato mixture and oil.
5 Cover dish with foil; bake in moderate oven 1 hour. Remove foil; bake in moderate oven about 30 minutes or until vegetables are tender. Sprinkle tiella with oregano leaves.

SERVES 8
per serving 7.6g fat; 675kJ (161 cal)

fennel and potato gratin

PREPARATION TIME 20 MINUTES   **COOKING TIME** 1 HOUR 15 MINUTES

A gratin is any recipe that uses a topping of breadcrumbs, cheese and small pieces of butter, which is then heated under a grill or in an oven until browned and crisp. You can also use spunta potatoes for this recipe.

800g sebago potatoes, peeled
2 small fennel (400g),
    sliced thinly
1 tablespoon plain flour
1¾ cups (430ml) cream
¼ cup (60ml) milk
20g butter
¾ cup (90g) coarsely grated
    cheddar cheese
¾ cup (50g) stale breadcrumbs

1 Preheat oven to moderate; oil deep 2-litre (8-cup) baking dish.
2 Using sharp knife, mandoline or V-slicer, cut potatoes into very thin slices; pat dry with absorbent paper. Layer a quarter of the potato slices into prepared dish; top with a third of the fennel. Continue layering remaining potato and fennel, finishing with potato.
3 Blend flour with a little of the cream in medium jug to form a smooth paste; stir in remaining cream and milk. Pour cream mixture over potato; dot with butter. Cover with foil; bake in moderate oven about 1 hour or until vegetables are just tender. Remove foil, top with combined cheese and breadcrumbs; bake, uncovered, about 15 minutes or until top is browned lightly.

SERVES 8
per serving 29.5g fat; 1548kJ (370 cal)
For a lower-fat version, use light cream, no-fat milk and reduced-fat cheddar cheese.
per serving 16.6g fat; 1102kJ (263 cal)

the perfect mash

PREPARATION TIME 10 MINUTES **COOKING TIME** 20 MINUTES

For the most lusciously smooth, fluffy, irresistible mash, this is the recipe to follow. Use potatoes that are high in starch and take care not to overcook them. Push the potato through a sieve, as we suggest here, or through a potato ricer or food mill (mouli).
You can also use pink-eye or sebago potatoes for this recipe.

1kg lasoda potatoes, peeled,
    cut into 3cm pieces
40g butter, softened
¾ cup (180ml) hot milk

1 Place potato in medium saucepan with enough cold water to barely cover the potato. Boil, uncovered, over medium heat about 15 minutes or until potato is tender. Drain.
2 Using the back of a wooden spoon, push potato through fine sieve into large bowl. Use same spoon to stir butter and hot milk into potato, folding gently until mash is smooth and fluffy.

SERVES 4
per serving 10.1g fat; 1011kJ (242 cal)
For a lower-fat version, use low-fat dairy-free spread instead of the butter, and no-fat milk.
per serving 4.2g fat; 794kJ (190 cal)

TIPS Satisfactory results can be had by mashing potato in a bowl with a traditional potato masher. Don't try to mash potato in a food processor as it will become gluey.
After potato is drained, work quickly, never allowing it to become cold. Heat any liquid ingredients you intend to stir into the mash.
Different potato varieties absorb different amounts of water when they are cooked, and the method of cooking (steaming, microwaving or boiling) also determines how much water is absorbed into the cooked potato. The age of the potato also has an effect on the amount of liquid it can absorb. Therefore, the amount of liquid needed for a perfect mash will vary. With practice, you should be able to tell by looking at a mash mixture when it has had the right amount of liquid added. We found that lasoda potatoes gave the smoothest and most delicious mash.

Use a wooden spoon to push the cooked potato through a fine sieve

A potato ricer is a good tool to use for making small amounts of mash

You can also use a food mill (mouli) to ensure mash is lump-free

potato and vegetable mashes

Each of these mashes is enough to serve 4 people as a side dish.

capsicum mash

Quarter 2 medium capsicums; discard seeds and membranes. Roast under grill or in very hot oven, skin-side up, until skin blisters and blackens. Cover capsicum pieces with plastic or paper 5 minutes. Peel away skin; chop capsicum coarsely. Blend or process capsicum until smooth. Meanwhile, boil, steam or microwave 1kg peeled, coarsely chopped lasoda potato until tender; drain. Mash potato in large bowl; stir in ½ cup hot cream and 20g softened butter. Add capsicum to mash; stir until combined.

per serving 17.8g fat; 1315kJ (314 cal)
For a lower-fat version, use low-fat dairy-free spread instead of the butter, and light cream.
per serving 9g fat; 1002kJ (239 cal)

broad bean mash

Shell 1kg fresh broad beans, discard pods. Boil, steam or microwave beans until just tender; drain. Peel away grey-coloured outer shells; blend or process beans until smooth. Stir in 2 tablespoons hot cream. Boil, steam or microwave 1kg peeled, coarsely chopped lasoda potato until tender; drain. Mash potato in large bowl; stir in mashed bean mixture, 40g melted butter and another 2 tablespoons hot cream.

per serving 17.5g fat; 1390kJ (332 cal)
For a lower-fat version, use low-fat dairy-free spread instead of the butter, and light cream.
per serving 8.9g fat; 1082kJ (259 cal)

kumara mash

Boil, steam or microwave 500g peeled, coarsely chopped lasoda potato and 500g peeled, coarsely chopped kumara, together, until tender; drain. Mash potato and kumara in large bowl; stir in ¼ cup hot chicken stock and 40g melted butter.

per serving 8.5g fat; 892kJ (213 cal)
For a lower-fat version, use low-fat dairy-free spread instead of the butter.
per serving 4.2g fat; 733kJ (175 cal)

fennel mash

Slice 1 large fennel thinly. Melt 60g butter in large frying pan; cook fennel, covered, over low heat, about 10 minutes or until fennel is very soft. Blend or process fennel until smooth. Meanwhile, boil, steam or microwave 1kg peeled, coarsely chopped lasoda potato until tender; drain. Mash potato in large bowl; stir in fennel mixture and ½ cup hot cream.

per serving 26g fat; 1631kJ (390 cal)
For a lower-fat version, use low-fat dairy-free spread instead of the butter, and light cream.
per serving 12.9g fat; 1160kJ (277 cal)

spinach mash

Boil, steam or microwave 1kg peeled, coarsely chopped lasoda potato until tender; drain. Meanwhile, boil, steam or microwave 220g spinach leaves until wilted; drain. Squeeze out excess liquid. Blend or process spinach with 40g softened butter until almost smooth. Mash potato in large bowl; stir in ½ cup hot cream and spinach mixture.

per serving 22g fat; 1438kJ (344 cal)
For a lower-fat version, use low-fat dairy-free spread instead of the butter, and light cream.
per serving 11g fat; 1047kJ (250 cal)

pea mash

Boil, steam or microwave 1kg peeled, coarsely chopped lasoda potato and 1½ cups frozen peas, separately, until tender; drain. Mash potato in large bowl; stir in ¾ cup hot milk and 50g softened butter. Using fork, mash peas in small bowl; stir into potato mixture.

per serving 12g fat; 1185kJ (283 cal)
For a lower-fat version, use low-fat dairy-free spread instead of the butter, and no-fat milk.
per serving 5.4g fat; 928kJ (222 cal)

celeriac mash

Boil, steam or microwave 800g peeled, coarsely chopped lasoda potato and 1kg peeled, coarsely chopped celeriac, separately, until tender; drain. Mash potato and celeriac in large bowl; stir in ½ cup hot cream and 60g softened butter.

per serving 26.2g fat; 1619kJ (387 cal)
For a lower-fat version, use low-fat dairy-free spread instead of the butter, and light cream.
per serving 13.1g fat; 1148kJ (274 cal)

pumpkin mash

Boil, steam or microwave 500g peeled, coarsely chopped lasoda potato and 500g peeled, coarsely chopped pumpkin together until tender; drain. Mash potato and pumpkin in large bowl; stir in 30g softened butter.

per serving 6.7g fat; 681kJ (163 cal)
For a lower-fat version, use low-fat dairy-free spread instead of the butter.
per serving 3.5g fat; 562kJ (134 cal)

basic mash with flavours from the pantry

PREPARATION TIME is approximately **10 MINUTES**, depending on the flavour variation.
COOKING TIME is **20 MINUTES**. Recipe, including one of flavour variations, **SERVES 4**.

1kg lasoda potatoes, peeled,
    chopped coarsely
50g butter, softened
½ cup (125ml) hot cream

1 Boil, steam or microwave potato until tender; drain.
2 Mash potato (see page 58), butter and cream in large bowl until
   smooth, stirring in one of the following flavour variations.

per serving 23.8g fat; 1480kJ (354 cal) without flavour variation
For lower-fat versions, use low-fat dairy-free spread instead of the butter,
and light cream.
per serving 11.8g fat; 1049kJ (251 cal) without flavour variation

- 4 cloves crushed roasted garlic

- 340g can asparagus, drained, chopped finely and combined
  with ¾ cup finely grated parmesan cheese

- 310g can creamed corn

- 2 teaspoons wasabi paste

- 1 tablespoon sun-dried tomato pesto

- 2 tablespoons basil pesto

- 180g can tuna chunks in springwater, drained, flaked

- 2 teaspoons sambal oelek

- ½ cup (150g) bottled apple sauce

TIPS Satisfactory results can be had by mashing potato in a bowl with a
traditional potato masher. Don't try to mash potato in a food processor as
it will become gluey.
After potato is drained, work quickly, never allowing it to become cold.

apple sauce

basil pesto

roasted garlic

creamed corn

tuna

sambal oelek

asparagus

sun-dried tomato

wasabi

gnocchi

PREPARATION TIME 30 MINUTES (PLUS REFRIGERATION TIME) **COOKING TIME** 25 MINUTES

Gnocchi should be light, delicate, pillow-like dumplings which virtually melt on the tongue – very addictive when made properly. We provide you with three different serving sauces (see opposite), but most of your favourite pasta sauces will suit gnocchi just as well. Each of the sauce recipes makes enough to accompany this gnocchi recipe.

1kg russet burbank
    potatoes, unpeeled
2 eggs, beaten lightly
30g butter, melted
¼ cup (20g) finely grated
    parmesan cheese
2 cups (300g) plain flour,
    approximately

1 Boil or steam whole potatoes until tender; drain. Peel when cool enough to handle. Mash, using ricer, food mill (mouli), or sieve and wooden spoon, into large bowl; stir in eggs, butter, parmesan and enough of the flour to make a firm dough.

2 Divide dough into eight equal parts; roll each part on lightly floured surface into 2cm-thick sausage-shape. Cut each sausage-shape into 2cm pieces; roll pieces into balls.

3 Roll each ball along the inside tines of a fork, pressing lightly on top of ball with index finger to form classic gnocchi shape, grooved on one side and dimpled on the other. Place gnocchi, in single layer, on lightly floured tray, cover; refrigerate 1 hour.

4 Cook gnocchi, uncovered, in large saucepan of boiling salted water about 3 minutes or until gnocchi float to the surface. Remove from pan with slotted spoon; drain. Serve hot, with the sauce of your choice.

SERVES 8
per serving 5.8g fat; 1079kJ (258 cal)

TIPS Add 1 teaspoon of any finely chopped herb you wish, such as rosemary, thyme, sage or oregano, to the gnocchi dough, if desired.
Potato should be mashed while hot but can be cooled slightly before being mixed with remaining ingredients.

Add enough of the flour to the mixture to make a firm dough

Use fingers to roll one part of dough into 2cm-thick sausage-shape

Roll each ball along the inside tines of a fork to form gnocchi shape

classic pesto

PREPARATION TIME 10 MINUTES **COOKING TIME** 5 MINUTES

2 cloves garlic, quartered
¼ cup (40g) toasted pine nuts
¼ cup (20g) finely grated parmesan cheese
1 cup firmly packed fresh basil leaves
⅓ cup (80ml) olive oil
½ cup (125ml) cream

1 Blend or process garlic, pine nuts, cheese and basil until finely chopped. With motor operating, gradually add oil until pesto is thick.

2 Just before serving, transfer pesto to small saucepan, add cream; stir, uncovered, over low heat until heated through.

per serving (without gnocchi) 20.5g fat; 807kJ (193 cal)

tomato sauce

PREPARATION TIME 10 MINUTES **COOKING TIME** 35 MINUTES

2 tablespoons olive oil
1 large brown onion (200g), chopped finely
2 cloves garlic, crushed
2 tablespoons tomato paste
2 x 425g cans crushed tomatoes
¼ cup finely shredded fresh basil leaves

1 Heat oil in medium heavy-base saucepan; cook onion and garlic, stirring, until onion softens.

2 Add tomato paste; cook, stirring, 1 minute. Stir in undrained tomatoes; bring to a boil. Reduce heat; simmer, uncovered, about 30 minutes or until sauce thickens slightly. Stir in basil.

per serving (without gnocchi) 5g fat; 299kJ (71 cal)

three-cheese sauce

PREPARATION TIME 10 MINUTES **COOKING TIME** 15 MINUTES

60g butter
⅓ cup (50g) plain flour
2 cups (500ml) milk
300ml cream
60g coarsely grated provolone cheese
70g coarsely grated fontina cheese
40g gorgonzola cheese, crumbled

1 Melt butter in medium saucepan. Add flour; cook, stirring, until mixture thickens and bubbles. Gradually add milk and cream; stir until mixture boils and thickens. Remove from heat; stir in cheeses.

per serving (without gnocchi) 31.1g fat; 1446kJ (345 cal)

TIP This sauce must be made just before serving.

potato crush

PREPARATION TIME is approximately 10 MINUTES, depending on the flavour variation.
COOKING TIME is 10 MINUTES. Recipe, including one of flavour variations, **SERVES 4**.

1kg tiny new potatoes, unpeeled
½ cup (120g) sour cream
40g butter, softened

1 Boil, steam or microwave whole potatoes until tender; drain.
2 Mash about half of the unpeeled whole potatoes (see page 58), sour cream and butter in large bowl until smooth; stir in one of the flavour variations opposite.
3 Using back of a fork or potato masher, gently crush remaining potatoes until skins burst and flesh is just flattened; fold into mash mixture.

Mash half of the potatoes with the sour cream and butter in a large bowl

Once the potato mash is smooth, stir in one of the flavour variations

Gently crush the remaining potatoes until skins burst and flesh is just flattened

kipfler crush

PREPARATION TIME 10 MINUTES **COOKING TIME** 20 MINUTES

1kg kipfler potatoes, unpeeled
40g butter, softened
½ cup (120g) sour cream
½ cup (125ml) hot milk

1 Boil, steam or microwave potatoes until tender; drain.
2 Mash about half of the unpeeled whole potatoes (see page 58), butter, sour cream and milk in large bowl until smooth; stir in one of the flavour variations at right, if desired.
3 Using back of a fork or potato masher, gently crush remaining potatoes until skins burst and flesh is just flattened; fold into mash mixture.

SERVES 4
per serving 21.6g fat; 1543kJ (369 cal)
For a lower-fat version, use low-fat dairy-free spread instead of the butter, light sour cream and no-fat milk.
per serving 10.1g fat; 1139kJ (272 cal)

original potato salad

Combine 6 coarsely chopped drained cornichons, 3 coarsely chopped green onions, ¼ cup coarsely chopped fresh flat-leaf parsley and 1 tablespoon coarsely chopped drained capers in small bowl.

per serving 20.4g fat; 1478kJ (353 cal)

For a lower-fat version, use low-fat dairy-free spread instead of the butter, and light sour cream.

per serving 10.1g fat; 1114kJ (266 cal)

caesar salad

Fry 3 finely chopped bacon rashers in non-stick frying pan until crisp; drain on absorbent paper. Combine with 4 finely chopped anchovies, 1 crushed garlic clove, 3 thinly sliced green onions and ½ cup shaved parmesan cheese in small bowl.

per serving 27.6g fat; 1905kJ (455 cal)

For a lower-fat version, use low-fat dairy-free spread instead of the butter, and light sour cream.

per serving 17.4g fat; 1541kJ (368 cal)

herb and mustard salad

Combine 1 tablespoon wholegrain mustard, ¼ cup coarsely chopped fresh chives, ¼ cup coarsely chopped fresh flat-leaf parsley, 2 tablespoons coarsely chopped fresh basil and 2 tablespoons coarsely chopped fresh dill in small bowl.

per serving 20.5g fat; 1475kJ (352 cal)

For a lower-fat version, use low-fat dairy-free spread instead of the butter, and light sour cream.

per serving 10.3g fat; 1111kJ (265 cal)

mashed potato casserole

PREPARATION TIME 10 MINUTES **COOKING TIME** 1 HOUR

You can also use coliban or nicola potatoes for this recipe.

500g sebago potatoes, peeled, chopped coarsely

30g butter, softened

2 eggs, beaten lightly

300ml cream

1 cup (120g) coarsely grated cheddar cheese

2 tablespoons coarsely chopped fresh chives

1 Boil, steam or microwave potato until tender; drain. Mash potato in large bowl with butter until smooth; spread over base of lightly oiled shallow 1.5-litre (6-cup) baking dish.

2 Preheat oven to moderate.

3 Combine remaining ingredients in medium bowl; pour over potato. Bake, uncovered, in moderate oven about 40 minutes or until top sets and is browned.

SERVES 4

per serving 51.1g fat; 2426kJ (580 cal)

For a lower-fat version, use low-fat dairy-free spread instead of the butter, light cream, reduced-fat cheddar cheese and no-fat milk.

per serving 28.9g fat; 1652kJ (395 cal)

baked creamed potatoes

PREPARATION TIME 20 MINUTES **COOKING TIME** 50 MINUTES

We used whole-egg mayonnaise. You can also use pink-eye or sebago potatoes for this recipe.

1kg lasoda potatoes, peeled, chopped coarsely

20g butter

3 bacon rashers (210g), rind removed, chopped finely

4 green onions, chopped finely

½ cup (150g) mayonnaise

½ cup (120g) sour cream

½ cup (125ml) cream

2 eggs, beaten lightly

1 tablespoon wholegrain mustard

¼ cup coarsely chopped fresh flat-leaf parsley

¾ cup (60g) finely grated parmesan cheese

1 Boil, steam or microwave potato until tender; drain.

2 Meanwhile, melt butter in medium frying pan; cook bacon and onion, stirring, until bacon is crisp.

3 Preheat oven to moderate.

4 Mash potato in large bowl with mayonnaise, sour cream and cream until smooth. Stir bacon mixture, eggs, mustard, parsley and ⅔ of the cheese into potato mixture. Spread mixture into lightly oiled shallow 1.75-litre (7-cup) baking dish; sprinkle with remaining cheese. Bake, uncovered, in moderate oven about 30 minutes or until top browns and potato mixture just sets.

SERVES 4
per serving 53.1g fat; 2989kJ (714 cal)
For a lower-fat version, use low-fat dairy-free spread instead of the butter, low-fat mayonnaise, light sour cream and light cream.
per serving 31.1g fat; 2196kJ (525 cal)

skordalia

PREPARATION TIME 15 MINUTES
COOKING TIME 15 MINUTES

Skordalia is a tangy Greek sauce or dip made with pureed potatoes and breadcrumbs or ground nuts (or, as in this case, both). Skordalia can be served with almost any kind of dish – from grilled meats and poultry to fish and raw vegetables.

400g russet burbank potatoes, peeled, chopped coarsely
2 slices white bread
½ cup (60g) almond meal
3 cloves garlic, crushed
2 tablespoons apple cider vinegar
⅓ cup (80ml) water
¼ cup (60ml) olive oil

1 Boil, steam or microwave potato until tender; drain. Mash potato in medium bowl.
2 Meanwhile, trim and discard crusts from bread. Soak bread in small bowl of cold water; drain. Squeeze out excess water.
3 Blend or process bread with almond meal, garlic, vinegar and the water until mixture is smooth. With motor operating, gradually add oil, processing until mixture thickens slightly. Fold bread mixture into potato mash.

MAKES 2 CUPS
per tablespoon 3.8g fat; 215kJ (51 cal)

colcannon

PREPARATION TIME 15 MINUTES   **COOKING TIME** 20 MINUTES

A hearty but meatless cabbage and potato dish served on Halloween in Ireland, colcannon traditionally had buried within its content a gold ring, coin, thimble and button. The diner who discovered the ring was supposed to marry within the year, while the coin symbolised wealth; the thimble and button meant that the people who found them would not marry.

1kg sebago potatoes, peeled,
   chopped coarsely
⅓ cup (80ml) hot cream
80g butter, softened
2 medium brown onions (300g),
   chopped finely
1 clove garlic, crushed
350g savoy cabbage,
   shredded finely

1 Boil, steam or microwave potato until tender; drain.
2 Using potato masher, mash potato, cream and half of the butter in medium bowl until mixture is smooth.
3 Melt remaining butter in large frying pan; cook onion and garlic, stirring, until onion softens. Add cabbage; cook, stirring, about 2 minutes or until cabbage just wilts. Fold potato mixture into cabbage mixture.

SERVES 4
per serving 25.4g fat; 1664kJ (397 cal)
For a lower-fat version, use light cream and low-fat dairy-free spread instead of the butter.
per serving 12.6g fat; 1197kJ (286 cal)

smoked fish pot pies

PREPARATION TIME 30 MINUTES **COOKING TIME** 35 MINUTES

You can also use lasoda or nicola potatoes for this recipe.

750g smoked cod fillets
2 cups (500ml) milk
1 bay leaf
6 black peppercorns
1kg coliban potatoes, peeled,
    chopped coarsely
50g butter, softened
20g butter, extra
1 large brown onion (200g),
    chopped finely
1 clove garlic, crushed
¼ cup (35g) plain flour
2½ cups (625ml) milk, extra
1 cup (120g) frozen peas
1 teaspoon finely grated
    lemon rind
2 tablespoons lemon juice
2 hard-boiled eggs, quartered

1 Place fish, milk, bay leaf and peppercorns in medium saucepan; bring to a boil. Reduce heat; simmer, uncovered, 10 minutes. Drain; discard liquid and spices. Using disposable kitchen gloves, remove and discard skin from fish; flake flesh into large chunks in medium bowl.

2 Meanwhile, boil, steam or microwave potato until tender; drain. Mash potato with softened butter in large bowl; cover to keep warm.

3 Melt extra butter in medium saucepan; cook onion and garlic, stirring, until onion softens. Add flour; cook, stirring, until mixture thickens and bubbles. Gradually add extra milk; stir until mixture boils and thickens. Add peas, rind and juice; remove from heat. Stir in fish.

4 Divide egg, fish mixture and potato mixture among four 2-cup (500ml) flameproof dishes. Place dishes on oven tray under very hot grill until tops are browned lightly.

SERVES 4
per serving 29.2g fat; 2910kJ (695 cal)
For a lower-fat version, use no-fat milk and low-fat dairy-free spread instead of the butter.
per serving 12.4g fat; 2349kJ (561 cal)

mash-filled cabbage rolls with cheesy cream sauce

PREPARATION TIME 25 MINUTES **COOKING TIME** 40 MINUTES

You can also use lasoda or pink-eye potatoes for this recipe.

1kg sebago potatoes, peeled, chopped coarsely
40g butter, softened
1 egg yolk
4 large cabbage leaves
4 bacon rashers (280g), rind removed, chopped coarsely
¼ cup (30g) coarsely grated cheddar cheese

cheesy cream sauce
20g butter
¼ cup (35g) plain flour
1½ cups (375ml) chicken stock
½ cup (125ml) cream
½ cup (60g) coarsely grated cheddar cheese
¼ cup finely chopped fresh flat-leaf parsley

1 Boil, steam or microwave potato until tender; drain. Mash potato in large bowl with butter and egg yolk.
2 Meanwhile, discard thick stems from cabbage. Boil, steam or microwave leaves until just pliable; drain. Rinse under cold water; drain. Pat dry with absorbent paper.
3 Preheat oven to moderately hot. Make cheesy cream sauce.
4 Place leaves, vein-side up, on board. Cut leaves in half lengthways; divide potato mixture evenly among leaf halves, placing mixture at stem end. Roll firmly, folding in sides to enclose filling.
5 Place cabbage rolls, seam-side down, in shallow lightly oiled 2-litre (8-cup) ovenproof dish; pour cheesy cream sauce over rolls, sprinkle with bacon and cheese. Bake, uncovered, in moderately hot oven about 20 minutes or until bacon is crisp and cabbage rolls are heated through.
cheesy cream sauce Melt butter in medium saucepan. Add flour; cook, stirring, until mixture thickens and bubbles. Gradually add stock and cream; stir until mixture boils and thickens. Stir in cheese and parsley.

SERVES 4
per serving 40.4g fat; 2521kJ (602 cal)
For a lower-fat version, use low-fat dairy-free spread instead of the butter, light cream and reduced-fat cheddar cheese.
per serving 25.1g fat; 1978kJ (473 cal)

cottage pie

PREPARATION TIME 20 MINUTES **COOKING TIME** 1 HOUR 35 MINUTES

1 tablespoon olive oil

2 cloves garlic, crushed

1 large brown onion (200g),
   chopped finely

2 medium carrots (240g), peeled,
   chopped finely

1kg beef mince

1 tablespoon worcestershire sauce

2 tablespoons tomato paste

2 x 425g cans crushed tomatoes

1 teaspoon dried mixed herbs

200g mushrooms, quartered

1 cup (120g) frozen peas

1kg sebago potatoes, peeled,
   chopped coarsely

¾ cup (180ml) hot milk

40g butter, softened

½ cup (50g) coarsely grated
   pizza cheese

1 Heat oil in large saucepan; cook garlic, onion and carrot, stirring, until onion softens. Add beef; cook, stirring, about 10 minutes or until changed in colour.

2 Add sauce, paste, undrained tomatoes and herbs; bring to a boil. Reduce heat; simmer, uncovered, about 30 minutes or until mixture thickens slightly. Stir in mushrooms and peas.

3 Meanwhile, preheat oven to moderate. Boil, steam or microwave potato until tender; drain. Mash potato in large bowl with milk and butter.

4 Pour beef mixture into deep 3-litre (12-cup) ovenproof dish; top with mashed potato mixture; sprinkle with cheese. Bake, uncovered, in moderate oven about 45 minutes or until pie is heated through and top is browned lightly.

SERVES 8
per serving 22.8g fat; 1816kJ (434 cal)
For a lower-fat version, use lean mince, no-fat milk, low-fat dairy-free spread instead of the butter, and reduced-fat cheddar cheese.
per serving 15.1g fat; 1590kJ (380 cal)

TIPS You can make the cottage pie up to 2 days in advance; keep, covered, in refrigerator. Reheat, covered, in moderately slow oven for about 40 minutes. The pie can also be frozen for up to 3 months; thaw overnight in the refrigerator before reheating as above.

duchesse potatoes

PREPARATION TIME 20 MINUTES **COOKING TIME** 40 MINUTES

You can also use coliban or lasoda potatoes for this recipe.

1kg nicola potatoes, peeled,
  chopped coarsely
3 egg yolks
100g butter, melted

1 Preheat oven to moderate; grease and line two oven trays.
2 Boil, steam or microwave potato until tender; drain. Mash potato in large bowl with egg yolks and butter.
3 Spoon potato mixture into large piping bag fitted with 1cm-fluted tube; pipe potato into 3cm rosette-shaped swirls onto prepared trays. Bake, uncovered, in moderate oven about 30 minutes or until browned lightly.

MAKES 40
per rosette 2.5g fat; 154kJ (37 cal)
For a lower-fat version, use low-fat dairy-free spread instead of the butter.
per rosette 1.4g fat; 114kJ (27 cal)

TIPS For a variation, stir ½ cup finely grated parmesan cheese into the potato with the egg yolks and butter.
The potato can be piped up to 3 hours ahead; keep, covered, in the refrigerator.

smoked salmon pie

PREPARATION TIME 10 MINUTES **COOKING TIME** 35 MINUTES

You can also use lasoda or sebago potatoes for this recipe.

1kg pink-eye potatoes, peeled, chopped coarsely
40g butter, softened
¼ cup (60g) sour cream
200g smoked salmon, chopped coarsely
2 eggs, separated
2 green onions, chopped finely

1 Preheat oven to moderately hot.
2 Boil, steam or microwave potato until tender; drain. Mash potato in large bowl with butter and sour cream. Stir in salmon, one of the egg yolks, egg whites and onion.
3 Spoon mixture into deep 22cm-round loose-base flan tin; smooth top with spatula, brush with remaining egg yolk. Bake, uncovered, in moderately hot oven about 25 minutes or until pie is heated through and browned lightly.

SERVES 6
per serving 12.9g fat; 1040kJ (248 cal)
For a lower-fat version, use low-fat dairy-free spread instead of butter, and light sour cream.
per serving 8g fat; 865kJ (207 cal)

stuffed portobello mushrooms

PREPARATION TIME 20 MINUTES **COOKING TIME** 20 MINUTES

500g lasoda potatoes, peeled,
  chopped coarsely
¼ cup (60ml) hot cream
20g butter, softened
8 large portobello
  mushrooms (400g)
30g butter, melted, extra
1 tablespoon olive oil
1 small brown onion (80g),
  chopped finely
2 cloves garlic, crushed
1 fresh small red thai chilli,
  seeded, chopped finely
1 cup (120g) coarsely grated
  cheddar cheese
¼ cup coarsely chopped fresh
  flat-leaf parsley
2 tablespoons finely chopped
  fresh chives
1 teaspoon fresh thyme leaves

1 Preheat oven to moderate.
2 Boil, steam or microwave potato
   until tender; drain. Mash potato
   in large bowl with cream and
   butter. Cover to keep warm.
3 Meanwhile, remove and reserve
   stems from mushrooms. Brush
   caps with extra butter; place,
   stem-side up, on oven tray. Bake,
   uncovered, in moderate oven for
   5 minutes; cover to keep warm.
4 Chop reserved stems finely.
   Heat oil in medium frying pan;
   cook onion, garlic, chilli and
   mushroom stems, stirring, until
   onion softens. Add cheese,
   parsley, chives and thyme;
   stir until combined.
5 Combine onion mixture with
   potato mixture; spoon mixture
   into mushroom caps.
6 Place caps on oven tray under
   hot grill about 5 minutes or until
   browned lightly.

SERVES 4
per serving 32g fat; 1729kJ (413 cal)
For a lower-fat version, use light cream, low-fat dairy-free spread instead
of the butter, and reduced-fat cheddar cheese.
per serving 20.5g fat; 1323kJ (316 cal)

TIP The portobello mushroom is virtually a larger version of the swiss brown
or cremini mushroom. Dense and hearty, it is a great variety to choose when
making stuffed mushrooms. You can use swiss browns here but purchase the
largest ones you can find.

vegetarian tarts

PREPARATION TIME 20 MINUTES **COOKING TIME** 25 MINUTES

You can also use nicola or sebago potatoes for this recipe.

1kg lasoda potatoes, peeled,
    chopped coarsely
½ cup (125ml) hot vegetable stock
30g butter
2 cloves garlic, crushed
200g mushrooms, sliced thickly
2 tablespoons finely shredded
    fresh basil
2 green onions, chopped finely
⅔ cup (80g) coarsely grated
    cheddar cheese
3 sheets fillo pastry
30g butter, melted

1 Boil, steam or microwave potato until tender; drain. Mash potato in large bowl with stock.
2 Meanwhile, melt butter in small frying pan; cook garlic and mushroom, stirring, until mushroom softens. Stir mushroom mixture, basil, onion and half of the cheese into potato mixture.
3 Preheat oven to moderately hot. Grease four 1-cup (250ml) metal pie dishes. Place a 2.5cm x 30cm strip of baking paper over base of each dish, extending 5cm over sides of dishes.
4 Stack fillo sheets; cut stack in half crossways. Brush between layers with melted butter, then cut stack into four squares. Line prepared dishes with squares. Spoon potato mixture into dishes; sprinkle with remaining cheese.
5 Place dishes on oven tray; bake tarts in moderately hot oven about 15 minutes or until pastry is browned lightly. Use baking paper strips to lift tarts out of pie dishes.

SERVES 4
per serving 19.9g fat; 1612kJ (385 cal)
For a lower-fat version, use low-fat dairy-free spread instead of the butter, and reduced-fat cheddar cheese.
per serving 11.5g fat; 1309kJ (313 cal)

special-occasion mash

PREPARATION TIME 10 MINUTES **COOKING TIME** 20 MINUTES

You can also use coliban or pink-eye potatoes for this recipe.

1kg sebago potatoes, peeled, chopped coarsely
1 cup (250g) mascarpone cheese
1 cup (80g) finely grated parmesan cheese
⅔ cup (80g) finely grated mozzarella cheese
½ cup (125ml) hot milk

1 Boil, steam or microwave potato until tender; drain.
2 Mash potato in large bowl with remaining ingredients.

SERVES 4
per serving 48.1g fat; 2646kJ (632 cal)
For a lower-fat version, use light cream cheese instead of the mascarpone, light mozzarella and no-fat milk.
per serving 20.6g fat; 1739kJ (415 cal)

potato dumplings with burnt butter

PREPARATION TIME 30 MINUTES **COOKING TIME** 45 MINUTES

You can also use lasoda or sebago potatoes for this recipe.

1kg pink-eye potatoes, unpeeled
1 clove garlic, crushed
50g butter, softened
2 eggs, beaten lightly
⅔ cup (100g) plain flour
¼ cup (20g) finely grated
    parmesan cheese
2 cups (500ml) water
1 litre (4 cups) chicken stock
125g butter, chopped
¼ cup loosely packed fresh
    sage leaves
1 teaspoon lemon juice

1 Boil, steam or microwave potatoes until tender; drain. Peel when cool enough to handle. Mash in large bowl with garlic and softened butter. Mix in eggs, flour and cheese, stirring, until mixture forms a soft dough.

2 Bring the water and stock to a boil in large saucepan. Reduce heat; cook rounded tablespoons of the dough, in batches, in simmering stock mixture about 4 minutes or until dumplings rise to the surface. Using slotted spoon, remove dumplings; divide dumplings among serving bowls.

3 Meanwhile, melt chopped butter in small frying pan; when butter just sizzles, cook sage until crisp, drain on absorbent paper. Reheat butter in same pan; stir over low heat until just browned. Remove from heat; stir in juice. Drizzle dumplings with burnt butter; top with crisp sage leaves.

SERVES 4
per serving 41.7g fat; 2646kJ (632 cal)

TIP Potato flour can be used in place of wheat flour for a gluten-free version.

potato puffs

PREPARATION TIME 15 MINUTES **COOKING TIME** 25 MINUTES

You can also use nicola or pink-eye potatoes for this recipe.

600g coliban potatoes, peeled, chopped coarsely
50g butter, softened
1 clove garlic, crushed
3 bacon rashers (210g), rind removed, chopped finely
½ cup (75g) self-raising flour
1 egg, beaten lightly
2 green onions, chopped finely
¾ cup (90g) finely grated gruyère cheese
vegetable oil, for deep-frying

1 Boil, steam or microwave potato until tender; drain. Mash potato in medium bowl with butter and garlic until smooth; cool.
2 Meanwhile, cook bacon in small non-stick frying pan until crisp; drain on absorbent paper. Add bacon, flour, egg, onion and cheese to potato mixture; stir until combined.
3 Heat oil in wok or large deep frying pan; deep-fry level tablespoons of the potato mixture, in batches, until browned. Drain on absorbent paper. Serve with sour cream, if desired.

MAKES 30
per puff 4.7g fat; 284kJ (68 cal)
For a lower-fat version, use low-fat dairy-free spread instead of the butter.
per puff 3.9g fat; 258kJ (62 cal)

TIP You can substitute 100g crumbled blue cheese for the gruyère, or add 310g can drained corn kernels for a delicious corn-flavoured potato puff.

the perfect potato salad

PREPARATION TIME 20 MINUTES (PLUS REFRIGERATION TIME) **COOKING TIME** 20 MINUTES

Crisp, low-starch potatoes, such as bintje, desiree, kipfler and sebago, make the best potato salad. Take care not to overcook them or they will break apart or crumble.

2kg sebago potatoes, peeled
2 tablespoons cider vinegar
8 green onions, sliced thinly
¼ cup finely chopped fresh flat-leaf parsley

mayonnaise
2 egg yolks
1 teaspoon dijon mustard
2 teaspoons lemon juice
1 cup (250ml) vegetable oil
2 tablespoons hot water, approximately

1 Cut potatoes into 1.5cm pieces. Place potato in large saucepan, barely cover with cold water; cover saucepan, bring to a boil. Reduce heat; simmer, uncovered, stirring occasionally, until just tender. Drain, spread potato on a tray; sprinkle with vinegar. Cool 10 minutes. Refrigerate, covered, until cold.

2 Meanwhile, make mayonnaise.

3 Place potato in large bowl with mayonnaise, onion and parsley; mix gently to combine.
mayonnaise Blend or process egg yolks, mustard and juice until smooth. With motor operating, gradually add oil in a thin, steady stream; process until mixture thickens. Add as much of the hot water as required to thin mayonnaise. Makes 1 cup.

SERVES 8
per serving 30.4g fat; 1727kJ (413 cal)
For a lower-fat version, use a commercial low-fat mayonnaise.
per serving 5.2g fat; 881kJ (210 cal)

After peeling the potatoes, cut them into approximately 1.5cm pieces

When the potato pieces are just tender, drain them in a colander

Spread the potato pieces on a tray, then drizzle with the cider vinegar

stuffed potatoes

Depending on what you decide to put in them, stuffed potatoes can make a light and healthy snack. We've given you these suggestions to indulge in, but use your favourite stuffing ideas if you prefer.

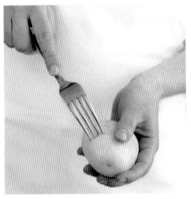
If microwaving raw potatoes, pierce skin of each with a fork to prevent it splitting

Using a sharp knife, cut a shallow slice from the top of each cooked potato

Using a teaspoon, carefully scoop out about two-thirds of the potato flesh

blue-cheese stuffed potatoes

PREPARATION TIME 15 MINUTES **COOKING TIME** 25 MINUTES

8 coliban potatoes (960g), unpeeled
80g firm blue-vein cheese, crumbled
125g packet cream cheese
½ cup (150g) mayonnaise
½ cup (120g) sour cream
1 clove garlic, quartered
⅓ cup (40g) coarsely chopped toasted pecans
2 teaspoons finely chopped fresh chives

1 Preheat oven to moderately hot. Lightly oil oven tray.
2 Boil, steam or microwave potatoes until just tender; drain.
3 Meanwhile, blend or process cheeses, mayonnaise, sour cream and garlic.
4 Cut shallow slice from top of each potato; using teaspoon, scoop flesh from each top into medium bowl, discard skin. Using teaspoon, carefully scoop about two-thirds of the flesh from each potato into same bowl; reserve potato shells.
5 Mash potato until smooth; stir in cheese mixture and half of the nuts. Place potato shells on prepared tray. Divide mixture among potato shells; bake, uncovered, in moderately hot oven about 15 minutes or until heated through. Top with remaining nuts and chives.

SERVES 4
per serving 48.3g fat; 2749kJ (657 cal)

chorizo stuffed potatoes

PREPARATION TIME 20 MINUTES
COOKING TIME 25 MINUTES

8 coliban potatoes (960g), unpeeled
1 teaspoon olive oil
70g chorizo sausage, chopped finely
1 clove garlic, crushed
1 cup (250g) canned crushed tomatoes
⅓ cup (90g) sour cream
2 tablespoons pizza cheese

1 Preheat oven to moderately hot. Lightly oil oven tray.
2 Boil, steam or microwave potatoes until tender; drain.
3 Meanwhile, heat oil in small frying pan; cook chorizo, stirring, about 3 minutes or until crisp. Drain on absorbent paper. Cook garlic in same pan, stirring over low heat, until just fragrant. Return chorizo to pan with undrained tomatoes; simmer, uncovered, until mixture reduces by half.
4 Cut shallow slice from top of each potato; using teaspoon, scoop flesh from each top into medium bowl, discard skin. Using teaspoon, carefully scoop about two-thirds of the flesh from each potato into same bowl; reserve potato shells.
5 Mash potato until smooth; stir in chorizo mixture and sour cream. Place potato shells on prepared tray. Divide mixture among potato shells, sprinkle with cheese; bake, uncovered, in moderately hot oven about 15 minutes or until heated through.

SERVES 4
per serving 16.3g fat; 1375kJ (328 cal)

creamed-corn stuffed potatoes

PREPARATION TIME 20 MINUTES
COOKING TIME 25 MINUTES

8 coliban potatoes (960g), unpeeled
1 teaspoon vegetable oil
30g sliced prosciutto, chopped coarsely
125g can creamed corn
2 tablespoons finely chopped fresh coriander

1 Preheat oven to moderately hot. Lightly oil oven tray.
2 Boil, steam or microwave potatoes until just tender; drain.
3 Meanwhile, heat oil in small frying pan; cook prosciutto, stirring, about 2 minutes or until crisp.
4 Cut shallow slice from top of each potato; using teaspoon, scoop flesh from each top into medium bowl, discard skin. Using teaspoon, carefully scoop about two-thirds of the flesh from each potato into same bowl; reserve potato shells.
5 Mash potato until smooth; stir in prosciutto, corn and coriander. Place potato shells on prepared tray. Divide mixture among potato shells; bake, uncovered, in moderately hot oven, about 15 minutes or until heated through.

SERVES 4
per serving 2.2g fat; 848kJ (203 cal)

parathas

PREPARATION TIME 40 MINUTES (PLUS STANDING TIME) **COOKING TIME** 30 MINUTES

Traditionally made with ghee and then cooked in ghee, our version uses butter in the pastry and is shallow-fried in vegetable oil. Parathas are best cooked just before serving. You can also use nicola or sebago potatoes for this recipe.

1 cup (150g) white plain flour
1 cup (160g) wholemeal
    plain flour
100g cold butter, chopped
½ cup (125ml) water
300g coliban potatoes, peeled,
    chopped coarsely
1 tablespoon peanut oil
1 small brown onion (80g),
    chopped finely
1 clove garlic, crushed
½ teaspoon ground cumin
1 teaspoon coriander
    seeds, crushed
¼ teaspoon cayenne pepper
1 tablespoon finely chopped
    fresh coriander
vegetable oil, for shallow-frying

1 Process flours and butter until mixture resembles fine breadcrumbs; add the water, pulse until mixture forms a soft dough. Wrap dough in plastic wrap; stand 1 hour.
2 Meanwhile, boil, steam or microwave potato until tender; drain. Mash in medium bowl.
3 Heat peanut oil in small frying pan; cook onion and garlic, stirring, until onion softens. Add cumin, crushed coriander and cayenne; cook, stirring, until fragrant. Add onion mixture to potato with fresh coriander; mix to combine. Cool filling 10 minutes.
4 Divide dough into 16 pieces. Roll eight pieces on lightly floured surface to form 14cm rounds (use a 14cm plate as a guide). Spread half of the filling over four of the rounds, leaving 1cm border; brush borders with water. Cover with remaining rounds; press edges together to seal. Repeat process with remaining eight dough pieces and filling.
5 Heat vegetable oil in medium frying pan; cook parathas, one at a time, until browned lightly both sides. Drain on absorbent paper; cover to keep warm.

MAKES 8
per paratha 19.8g fat; 1368kJ (327 cal)

TIP When you're rolling individual parathas, cover the remaining dough with a damp tea towel to stop it drying out.

On a lightly floured surface, roll each piece of the dough into a 14cm round

Use a 14cm plate as a guide to trim the dough into a circle

Brush the border with water before topping it with another round

potato patties with vegetable ragoût

PREPARATION TIME 25 MINUTES (PLUS REFRIGERATION TIME) **COOKING TIME** 35 MINUTES

Ragoût, which comes from the French verb, ragoûter, *meaning "to stimulate the appetite", does exactly that in this dish. You can also use lasoda or nicola potatoes for this recipe.*

1kg coliban potatoes, peeled, chopped coarsely
1 teaspoon olive oil
1 small brown onion (80g), chopped finely
1 clove garlic, crushed
1 egg, beaten lightly
1 tablespoon coarsely chopped fresh flat-leaf parsley
50g butter
2 tablespoons olive oil, extra

vegetable ragoût
30g butter
1 tablespoon olive oil
1 clove garlic, crushed
1 small brown onion (80g), chopped coarsely
2 trimmed celery sticks (150g), chopped coarsely
1 medium zucchini (120g), chopped coarsely
150g mushrooms, quartered
¼ cup (60ml) dry white wine
1 cup (260g) bottled tomato pasta sauce
½ cup (125ml) vegetable stock
½ cup (75g) seeded kalamata olives
2 tablespoons coarsely chopped fresh flat-leaf parsley

1 Boil, steam or microwave potato until just tender; drain. Mash roughly in large bowl.
2 Meanwhile, heat oil in small frying pan; cook onion and garlic, stirring, until onion softens.
3 Add onion mixture to potato with egg and parsley; stir to combine. Refrigerate 1 hour.
4 Meanwhile, make vegetable ragoût.
5 Using floured hands, shape potato mixture into eight patties. Heat butter and extra oil in large frying pan; cook patties, in batches, until browned lightly both sides. Serve patties with vegetable ragoût.
   vegetable ragoût Heat butter and oil in medium saucepan; cook garlic, onion and celery, stirring, until vegetables soften. Add zucchini and mushrooms; cook, stirring, 2 minutes. Add wine; cook, stirring, 1 minute. Add sauce, stock and olives; bring to a boil. Reduce heat; simmer, uncovered, about 10 minutes or until vegetables are cooked through. Remove from heat; stir in parsley.

SERVES 4
per serving 32.9g fat; 2143kJ (512 cal)

aloo gobi

PREPARATION TIME 15 MINUTES **COOKING TIME** 30 MINUTES

Aloo means potato and gobi, cauliflower, to an Indian cook, but this easy-to-make dry curry means delicious in anyone's vocabulary.

450g ruby lou potatoes, peeled, chopped coarsely
1 tablespoon (20g) ghee
1 tablespoon black mustard seeds
1 tablespoon cumin seeds
3 cloves garlic, crushed
½ teaspoon ground turmeric
½ teaspoon garam masala
1 large brown onion (200g), sliced thinly
2 medium tomatoes (380g), chopped coarsely
1kg cauliflower, chopped coarsely
1 cup (250ml) water
¼ cup loosely packed fresh coriander leaves

1 Boil, steam or microwave potato until just tender; drain.
2 Meanwhile, melt ghee in large saucepan; cook seeds, stirring, until they begin to pop. Add garlic, turmeric and garam masala; cook, stirring, until mixture is fragrant. Add onion; cook, stirring, until onion softens. Add tomato and cauliflower; cook, stirring, 1 minute.
3 Stir in the water; bring to a boil. Reduce heat; simmer, covered, 10 minutes. Stir in potato; simmer, covered, about 5 minutes or until vegetables are tender. Remove from heat; stir in coriander.

SERVES 4
per serving 6.6g fat; 829kJ (198 cal)

spanish tortilla

PREPARATION TIME 15 MINUTES **COOKING TIME** 30 MINUTES

You can also use bintje or pink fir apple potatoes for this recipe.

800g russet burbank potatoes, peeled, sliced thinly
1 tablespoon olive oil
1 large brown onion (200g), sliced thinly
200g chorizo sausage, sliced thinly
6 eggs, beaten lightly
300ml cream
4 green onions, sliced thickly
¼ cup (25g) coarsely grated mozzarella cheese
¼ cup (30g) coarsely grated cheddar cheese

1 Boil, steam or microwave potato until just tender; drain.
2 Meanwhile, heat oil in medium frying pan; cook brown onion, stirring, until softened. Add chorizo; cook, stirring, until crisp. Drain chorizo mixture on absorbent paper.
3 Whisk eggs in large bowl with cream, green onion and cheeses; stir in potato and chorizo mixture.
4 Pour mixture into heated lightly oiled medium non-stick frying pan; cook, covered, over low heat about 10 minutes or until tortilla is just set. Carefully invert tortilla onto plate, then slide back into pan; cook, uncovered, about 5 minutes or until cooked through.

SERVES 4
per serving 62.8g fat; 3241kJ (774 cal)
For a lower-fat version, use light cream and omit the cheese.
per serving 42.8g fat; 2477kJ (592 cal)

potato and beef pasties

PREPARATION TIME 30 MINUTES **COOKING TIME** 45 MINUTES

You can also use pink-eye or sebago potatoes for this recipe.

500g coliban potatoes, peeled, chopped coarsely
1 tablespoon olive oil
1 small brown onion (80g), chopped finely
2 cloves garlic, crushed
1 medium carrot (120g), chopped finely
1 trimmed celery stick (75g), chopped finely
350g beef mince
⅓ cup (80ml) dry red wine
1 cup (250ml) beef stock
¼ cup (70g) tomato paste
½ cup (60g) frozen peas
8 sheets ready-rolled puff pastry, thawed
1 egg, beaten lightly

1. Boil, steam or microwave potato until tender; drain. Mash in medium bowl.
2. Meanwhile, heat oil in medium saucepan; cook onion and garlic, stirring, until onion softens. Add carrot and celery; cook, stirring, until vegetables are tender. Add beef; cook, stirring, until changed in colour.
3. Stir in wine, stock, paste and peas; cook, uncovered, about 5 minutes or until mixture thickens slightly. Stir potato into beef mixture; cool 10 minutes.
4. Preheat oven to moderate. Lightly oil two oven trays.
5. Cut two 14cm-rounds from one pastry sheet; place rounds on oven tray. Place about ¹⁄₁₆ of the filling in centre of each round. Brush edge of pastry with egg; fold over to enclose filling, pressing around edge with fork to seal. Repeat process with remaining pastry sheets, one at a time as above, and remaining filling.
6. Bake pasties, uncovered, in moderate oven about 30 minutes or until browned lightly.

MAKES 16
per pasty 8.5g fat; 656kJ (157 cal)

bubble and squeak

PREPARATION TIME 10 MINUTES **COOKING TIME** 30 MINUTES

Originally an English dish made from the leftovers of a roast dinner, usually cabbage, potatoes and – if any remained – meat, bubble and squeak's name is supposedly derived from the sounds the ingredients make while being tossed together in a frying pan. You can also use lasoda or sebago potatoes for this recipe.

450g nadine potatoes, peeled, chopped coarsely
250g cabbage, chopped coarsely
4 bacon rashers (280g), rind removed, chopped coarsely
1 medium brown onion (150g), chopped coarsely

1 Boil, steam or microwave potato and cabbage, separately, until just tender; drain. Mash potato in medium bowl until smooth.
2 Meanwhile, cook bacon in large heated non-stick frying pan, stirring, until crisp; drain on absorbent paper.
3 Cook onion in same pan, stirring, until softened. Add potato, cabbage and bacon; stir to combine. Flatten mixture to form large cake-shape; cook, uncovered, until bottom of cake is just browned. Carefully invert onto plate, then slide back into frying pan; cook, uncovered, until browned on other side.

SERVES 4
per serving 5.1g fat; 649kJ (155 cal)

piroshki

PREPARATION TIME 30 MINUTES
(PLUS STANDING TIME)
COOKING TIME 30 MINUTES

*Piroshki are small Russian
dumplings that can have various
savoury or sweet fillings but this
one is among the most traditional.
Baked or fried, they make excellent
hors d'oeuvres.*

6 cups plain flour (900g)
1 tablespoon dry yeast (12g)
1 tablespoon salt
⅓ cup (75g) caster sugar
2 egg yolks
2 cups (500ml) milk, warmed
250g butter, melted
1 egg, beaten lightly

filling
1 tablespoon olive oil
1 medium brown onion (150g),
   chopped finely
1 clove garlic, crushed
250g sebago potatoes, peeled,
   chopped finely
2 bacon rashers (140g), rind
   removed, chopped finely
400g beef mince
⅓ cup (90g) tomato paste
2 teaspoons fresh thyme leaves

1 Combine flour, yeast, salt and sugar in large bowl. Make a well in the
centre; using hand, mix in egg yolks, milk and butter until mixture is soft
and elastic. Scrape down sides of bowl, cover; stand in warm place about
1 hour or until dough doubles in size.
2 Meanwhile, make the filling.
3 Turn dough onto floured surface; knead until smooth. Divide dough into
16 pieces; press each piece into 12cm round.
4 Preheat oven to hot. Lightly oil two oven trays.
5 Place rounded tablespoon of the filling in centre of each round; gather
edges, pinch firmly to enclose filling. Place piroshki, pinched-side down,
on prepared trays; brush with egg. Stand, uncovered, in warm place
15 minutes. Bake, uncovered, in hot oven about 15 minutes or until
golden brown.
filling Heat oil in large frying pan; cook onion, garlic, potato and bacon,
stirring, until potato softens. Add beef; cook, stirring, until changed in
colour. Stir in paste and thyme. Cool 10 minutes.

MAKES 16

per piroshki 20.3g fat; 1852kJ (442 cal)
For a lower-fat version, use no-fat milk and low-fat dairy-free spread
instead of the butter.
per piroshki 12.5g fat; 1563kJ (373 cal)

samosas

PREPARATION TIME 40 MINUTES (PLUS REFRIGERATION TIME) **COOKING TIME** 20 MINUTES

You can also use nicola or pink-eye potatoes for this recipe.

1½ cups (225g) plain flour
1 tablespoon ghee
1 tablespoon cumin seeds
½ cup (125ml) warm water,
    approximately
vegetable oil, for deep-frying

potato masala filling
125g coliban potatoes, peeled,
    chopped finely
1 teaspoon ghee
½ small brown onion (40g),
    chopped finely
1 clove garlic, crushed
½ fresh large green chilli, seeded,
    chopped finely
1 teaspoon grated fresh ginger
¼ teaspoon coriander seeds
¼ teaspoon cumin seeds
½ teaspoon garam masala
1 tablespoon finely chopped
    fresh coriander
1 teaspoon lemon juice

1 Place flour in medium bowl; rub in ghee. Add seeds; gradually stir in enough of the water to make a firm dough. Knead on floured surface until smooth and elastic, cover with plastic wrap; refrigerate 30 minutes.
2 Make potato masala filling.
3 Roll dough on lightly floured surface until 2mm thick; cut 28 x 8cm rounds from dough. Place level teaspoons of cold filling in centre of each round; brush around edge of rounds with water, press together to enclose filling.
4 Heat oil in large saucepan; deep-fry samosas, in batches, until browned and crisp. Drain on absorbent paper.
    potato masala filling Boil, steam or microwave potato until just tender; drain. Mash half of the potato in small bowl. Melt ghee in medium saucepan; cook onion, garlic, chilli, ginger, seeds and spices, stirring, until onion softens. Stir in coriander, juice and both mashed and chopped potato.

MAKES 28
per samosa 2.1g fat; 207kJ (49 cal)

white fish brandade

PREPARATION TIME 15 MINUTES (PLUS REFRIGERATION TIME) COOKING TIME 10 MINUTES

While a classic French brandade is based on salt cod, it can be made with any fish, flaked into a garlicky sauce. We used ling here, and the resultant take on the traditional is not only just as good but easier to prepare too.

200g sebago potatoes, peeled,
    chopped coarsely
2 cups (500ml) milk
350g white fish fillet,
    skinless, boneless
1 small white onion (80g),
    chopped coarsely
2 cloves garlic, quartered
2 tablespoons olive oil
2 tablespoons lemon juice
¼ cup (60g) sour cream

1 Boil, steam or microwave potato until tender; drain. Cool.
2 Meanwhile, bring milk to a boil in large non-stick frying pan; add fish, return to boil. Reduce heat; simmer, uncovered, until fish is cooked through, turning once during cooking.
3 When fish is cool enough to handle, break up over food processor or blender; process with potato and remaining ingredients until mixture forms a smooth paste. Place brandade in serving bowl, cover; refrigerate 30 minutes. Serve with crusty bread, if desired.

MAKES 2 CUPS
per tablespoon 1.3g fat; 89kJ (21 cal)
For a lower-fat version, use no-fat milk.
per tablespoon 1g fat; 79kJ (19 cal)

raclette

PREPARATION TIME 10 MINUTES
COOKING TIME 20 MINUTES

Like fondue, raclette is a staple winter meal in Switzerland and is traditionally made with the pungent Swiss melting cheese of the same name. You can substitute raclette with gruyère, appenzeller or even emmental.

4 coliban potatoes (680g),
   unpeeled
1 cup (125g) coarsely grated
   raclette cheese
20g butter
1 tablespoon coarsely chopped
   fresh flat-leaf parsley
½ cup (90g) drained cornichons
½ cup (100g) drained pickled
   cocktail onions

1 Boil, steam or microwave potatoes until tender; drain.
2 Cut a cross in each potato, taking care not to cut all the way through; gently squeeze potatoes open. Divide cheese among potatoes; top with butter.
3 Place potatoes under hot grill until cheese and butter melt. Sprinkle with parsley; serve with cornichons and onions.

SERVES 4
per serving 13.7g fat; 1171kJ (280 cal)

roast potato and bacon quiche

PREPARATION TIME 20 MINUTES **COOKING TIME** 1 HOUR 5 MINUTES

You can also use russet burbank or coliban potatoes for this recipe.

300g ruby lou potatoes, peeled, chopped coarsely
1 tablespoon olive oil
1 sheet ready-rolled puff pastry, thawed
2 teaspoons olive oil, extra
1 small brown onion (80g), sliced thinly
2 cloves garlic, crushed
3 bacon rashers (210g), rind removed, chopped coarsely
⅓ cup (80ml) milk
⅓ cup (80ml) cream
2 eggs
¼ cup (25g) coarsely grated mozzarella cheese

1 Preheat oven to moderately hot.
2 Place potato and oil in medium baking dish; stir to coat potato with oil. Roast, uncovered, in moderately hot oven about 30 minutes or until browned lightly and cooked through.
3 Meanwhile, cut pastry into four squares; gently press one square into each of four 1-cup (250ml) ovenproof dishes. Place dishes on oven tray; bake in moderately hot oven 10 minutes.
4 Heat extra oil in medium frying pan; cook onion, garlic and bacon, stirring, until onion softens and bacon is crisp. Drain on absorbent paper.
5 Divide potato among pastry shells; top with bacon mixture. Pour combined milk, cream, eggs and cheese into dishes. Bake, uncovered, in moderately hot oven about 30 minutes or until quiche filling sets. Stand 5 minutes; carefully remove quiches from dishes.

SERVES 4
per serving 26.5g fat; 1466kJ (350 cal)
For a lower-fat version, use no-fat milk, light cream and light mozzarella.
per serving 21.2g fat; 1287kJ (307 cal)

rosemary and potato pizza

PREPARATION TIME 20 MINUTES **COOKING TIME** 40 MINUTES

You can also use lasoda or nicola potatoes for this recipe.

3 medium pontiac potatoes
   (630g), unpeeled
1 teaspoon fresh rosemary leaves
2 tablespoons olive oil
1 cup (150g) self-raising flour
1 cup (150g) plain flour
30g butter
1 egg, beaten lightly
⅓ cup (80ml) milk
½ cup (40g) finely grated
   parmesan cheese
2 cloves garlic, crushed

1 Peel and coarsely chop one of the potatoes; boil, steam or microwave until tender, drain. Mash in small bowl; reserve ½ cup (110g) mashed potato. Using sharp knife, mandoline or V-slicer, cut remaining potatoes into 1mm slices. Pat dry with absorbent paper. Combine sliced potato in medium bowl with rosemary and oil.

2 Preheat oven to moderately hot. Lightly grease 25cm x 30cm swiss roll pan.

3 Combine flours in large bowl; using fingertips, rub butter into flour until mixture resembles fine breadcrumbs. Add mashed potato, egg and milk; stir until combined. Turn dough onto floured surface; knead until smooth.

4 Roll dough into 25cm x 30cm rectangle; carefully lift onto prepared pan. Using palm of hand, press dough into corners of pan to ensure base is covered evenly. Top pizza base with cheese and garlic; layer potato slices, overlapping slightly, over base. Bake, uncovered, in moderately hot oven about 30 minutes or until potato is tender and pizza is browned lightly.

SERVES 8
per serving 11g fat; 1207kJ (288 cal)
For a lower-fat version, use low-fat dairy-free spread instead of the butter, and no-fat milk.
per serving 9.1g fat; 1135kJ (271 cal)

curried potato soup

PREPARATION TIME 15 MINUTES **COOKING TIME** 35 MINUTES

You can also use desiree or ruby lou potatoes for this recipe.

30g butter
2 tablespoons vegetable oil
1 large brown onion (200g),
  chopped coarsely
2 cloves garlic, crushed
1 teaspoon garam masala
½ teaspoon ground turmeric
1 teaspoon ground cumin
1 teaspoon ground coriander
800g coliban potatoes, peeled,
  chopped coarsely
1 litre (4 cups) chicken stock
1½ cups (375ml) water
1 medium brown onion (150g),
  sliced thinly
½ cup (140g) yogurt

1 Heat butter and half of the oil in large saucepan; cook chopped onion and garlic, stirring, until onion softens. Add combined spices; cook, stirring, until fragrant. Add potato, stock and the water; bring to a boil. Reduce heat; simmer, covered, until potato is just tender. Cool 10 minutes.

2 Meanwhile, heat remaining oil in small frying pan; cook sliced onion, stirring, until browned and crisp. Drain on absorbent paper.

3 Blend or process soup, in batches, until smooth. Divide among serving bowls; top with yogurt and fried onion.

SERVES 6
per serving 12.1g fat; 915kJ (219 cal)
For a lower-fat version, use low-fat dairy-free spread instead of the butter, and low-fat yogurt.
per serving 9.2g fat; 817kJ (195 cal)

bacon and potato soup

PREPARATION TIME 15 MINUTES **COOKING TIME** 30 MINUTES

You can also use bintje or pink fir apple potatoes for this recipe.

6 bacon rashers (420g), rind
    removed, chopped coarsely
4 cloves garlic, crushed
1kg king edward potatoes, peeled,
    chopped coarsely
1 cup (250ml) chicken stock
2 cups (500ml) water
1¼ cups (300g) sour cream
¼ cup finely chopped fresh
    flat-leaf parsley

1 Cook bacon and garlic, stirring, in large heated
  saucepan until bacon is crisp.
2 Add potato, stock and the water; bring to a boil.
  Reduce heat; simmer, covered, until potato is just
  tender. Add sour cream; stir until heated through
  (do not boil). Remove from heat; stir in parsley.

SERVES 6

per serving 25.2g fat; 1567kJ (374 cal)
For a lower-fat version, use light sour cream.
per serving 15.1g fat; 1157kJ (276 cal).

corn chowder

PREPARATION TIME 20 MINUTES **COOKING TIME** 30 MINUTES

You can also use bintje or ruby lou potatoes for this recipe.

40g butter

1 clove garlic, crushed

1 medium leek (350g), trimmed, sliced thinly

½ cup (125ml) dry white wine

2 trimmed celery sticks (150g), chopped finely

800g desiree potatoes, peeled, chopped coarsely

2 cups (500ml) chicken stock

2 cups (500ml) water

2 cups (320g) frozen corn kernels

½ cup (125ml) cream

1 tablespoon finely chopped fresh flat-leaf parsley

1 Melt butter in large saucepan; cook garlic and leek, stirring, until leek softens. Add wine; cook, stirring, until liquid reduces by half. Add celery, potato, stock and the water; bring to a boil. Reduce heat; simmer, covered, until potato is just tender. Cool 10 minutes.

2 Blend or process 3 cups of the soup, in batches, until smooth. Return blended soup to remaining unprocessed soup; add corn and cream. Bring to a boil. Reduce heat; simmer, stirring, until corn is just tender. Remove from heat; stir in parsley.

SERVES 6
per serving 15.7g fat; 1217kJ (291 cal)
For a lower-fat version, use low-fat dairy-free spread instead of the butter, and light cream.
per serving 8.4g fat; 956kJ (228 cal)

vichyssoise

PREPARATION TIME 20 MINUTES (PLUS REFRIGERATION TIME) COOKING TIME 50 MINUTES

Vichyssoise is that classic French creamy potato and leek soup which is generally served cold. You can also use desiree or pink fir apple potatoes for this recipe.

50g butter
2 medium leeks (700g), trimmed, sliced thinly
750g coliban potatoes, peeled, chopped coarsely
2 cups (500ml) chicken stock
2 cups (500ml) water
300ml cream
2 tablespoons coarsely chopped fresh chives

1 Melt butter in large saucepan; cook leek, covered, about 20 minutes or until softened, stirring occasionally (do not allow leek to brown).
2 Add potato, stock and the water; bring to a boil. Reduce heat; simmer, covered, until potato is tender. Cool 10 minutes.
3 Blend or process soup, in batches, until smooth; place soup in large bowl. Stir in cream, cover; refrigerate 3 hours or overnight. Divide among serving bowls; sprinkle with chives just before serving.

SERVES 6
per serving 28.9g fat; 1486kJ (355 cal)
For a lower-fat version, use low-fat dairy-free spread instead of the butter, and light cream.
per serving 14.7g fat; 981kJ (234 cal)

potato, capsicum and chilli frittata

PREPARATION TIME 20 MINUTES **COOKING TIME** 25 MINUTES

You can also use desiree or ruby lou potatoes for this recipe.

1kg purple congo potatoes, peeled, sliced thickly
2 tablespoons olive oil
1 large red capsicum (350g), sliced thickly
1 large yellow capsicum (350g), sliced thickly
1 fresh small red thai chilli, chopped finely
10 eggs, beaten lightly
2 tablespoons coarsely chopped fresh coriander
½ cup (65g) grated pizza cheese
⅓ cup loosely packed fresh coriander leaves

1 Boil, steam or microwave potato until just tender; drain.
2 Meanwhile, heat half of the oil in 26cm flameproof frying pan; cook capsicums and chilli, stirring, about 5 minutes or until capsicums soften. Transfer capsicum mixture to small bowl.
3 Heat remaining oil in same pan; remove from heat. Layer half of the potato in pan; top with half of the capsicum. Repeat process with remaining potato and capsicum. Pour combined egg and chopped coriander carefully over vegetables; sprinkle with cheese. Cook, uncovered, over low heat, about 8 minutes or until base of frittata is just browned.
4 Place frittata under hot grill until top is just browned and frittata is set. Cut into wedges; sprinkle with coriander leaves.

SERVES 6
per serving 17.8g fat; 1375kJ (328 cal)

potato soufflés

PREPARATION TIME 15 MINUTES **COOKING TIME** 40 MINUTES

You can also use lasoda or sebago potatoes for this recipe.

350g desiree potatoes, peeled, chopped coarsely
2 tablespoons packaged breadcrumbs
60g butter
2 tablespoons plain flour
¾ cup (180ml) milk
3 eggs, separated
⅓ cup (90g) coarsely grated cheddar cheese
1 teaspoon fresh thyme leaves

1 Boil, steam or microwave potato until tender; drain. Mash potato in large bowl.

2 Preheat oven to moderately hot. Grease four ¾-cup (180ml) soufflé dishes; sprinkle bases and sides with breadcrumbs, shake out excess. Place prepared dishes on oven tray.

3 Melt butter in medium saucepan; cook flour, stirring, until mixture thickens and bubbles. Gradually add milk, stirring until mixture boils and thickens; remove from heat. Stir in egg yolks, cheese, thyme and potato, mixing until cheese melts and mixture is smooth. Return soufflé mixture to same large bowl.

4 Using electric mixer, beat egg whites in small bowl until soft peaks form. Fold egg whites, in two batches, into soufflé mixture. Spoon soufflé mixture into prepared dishes; bake, uncovered, in moderately hot oven about 20 minutes or until browned lightly and puffed.

SERVES 4
per serving 25.9g fat; 1637kJ (391 cal)
For a lower-fat version, use low-fat dairy-free spread instead of the butter, no-fat milk and reduced-fat cheddar cheese.
per serving 15.6g fat; 1268kJ (303 cal)

potato, olive and sun-dried tomato bread

PREPARATION TIME 15 MINUTES **COOKING TIME** 1 HOUR

You can also use nicola or pink-eye potatoes for this recipe.

250g coliban potatoes, peeled, chopped coarsely

30g butter, melted

2 cups (300g) self-raising flour

1 cup (250ml) milk

½ cup (60g) seeded green olives, sliced thickly

½ cup (75g) drained sun-dried tomatoes, sliced thickly

1 cup (100g) coarsely grated mozzarella cheese

1 Preheat oven to moderately hot. Grease 14cm x 21cm loaf pan; line base with baking paper.

2 Boil, steam or microwave potato until tender; drain. Mash potato in large bowl with butter until smooth.

3 Add flour, milk, olives, tomato and cheese to potato mixture; mix to combine. Spoon into prepared pan; bake, uncovered, in moderately hot oven about 50 minutes or until cooked through.

SERVES 8
per serving 8.3g fat; 1093kJ (261 cal)

boxty

Believed to have originated during the Irish famine, boxty is made of a mixture of mashed and grated potato and shaped into a thick pancake. You can also use lasoda or sebago potatoes for this recipe.

900g nadine potatoes, peeled
100g butter
1 clove garlic, crushed
3 cups (450g) self-raising flour
1 tablespoon milk
2 teaspoons sesame seeds

1 Boil, steam or microwave half of the potatoes; drain. Mash cooked potatoes in large bowl until smooth. Coarsely grate remaining raw potatoes.
2 Preheat oven to moderate. Line two oven trays with baking paper.
3 Add butter, garlic, flour and grated potato to mashed potato; mix until mixture forms a dough.
4 Knead dough on lightly floured surface; divide into quarters. Using hands, shape each quarter into 20cm round; score a shallow cross into top of each round.
5 Place rounds on prepared trays; brush with milk, sprinkle evenly with sesame seeds. Bake, uncovered, in moderate oven 20 minutes. Cover with foil; bake in moderate oven about 20 minutes or until cooked through.

SERVES 4
per serving 23.1g fat; 2925kJ (699 cal)
For a lower-fat version, use low-fat dairy-free spread instead of the butter.
per serving 12.3g fat; 2521kJ (602 cal)

chinese potato salad

PREPARATION TIME 20 MINUTES **COOKING TIME** 15 MINUTES

*Purple shallots are often found under the name of thai, asian
or even pink shallots; used throughout South-East Asia, they are a
member of the onion family but resemble garlic in that they grow in
multiple-clove bulbs and are intensely flavoured. They can be eaten
fresh in salads or can be deep-fried and served as a condiment.*

1kg pontiac potatoes, quartered
8 green onions, sliced thinly
5 purple shallots, sliced thinly
½ cup loosely packed fresh
  coriander leaves
½ cup coarsely chopped
  fresh mint
2 fresh small red thai chillies,
  seeded, sliced thinly

sesame lime dressing
¼ cup (60ml) lime juice
1 egg yolk
1 teaspoon sesame oil
¾ cup (180ml) peanut oil
2 teaspoons mirin
2 tablespoons finely chopped
  fresh coriander

1 Boil, steam or microwave potato
until just tender; drain. Make
sesame lime dressing.
2 Place remaining ingredients in
large bowl with warm potato
and sesame lime dressing; toss
gently to combine.
sesame lime dressing Blend
or process 1 tablespoon of the
juice with egg yolk until slightly
thickened. Gradually add oils in a
thin, steady stream; process until
mixture thickens. Stir in remaining
juice and remaining ingredients.

SERVES 4
per serving 45.7g fat;
2332kJ (557 cal)

satay chicken potato salad

PREPARATION TIME 20 MINUTES **COOKING TIME** 15 MINUTES

*You need a medium barbecued chicken for this recipe; discard skin
and bones before chopping the meat. This salad can be served warm
or cold. You can also use bintje or pink fir apple potatoes for this recipe.*

1kg nicola potatoes, unpeeled,
    cut into wedges
2½ cups (400g) thinly sliced
    cooked chicken
6 green onions, sliced thinly
60g baby spinach
    leaves, trimmed
½ cup (70g) roasted
    unsalted peanuts
½ cup (150g) satay sauce
½ cup (120g) sour cream
1 tablespoon hot water

1 Boil, steam or microwave potato
  until just tender; drain.
2 Combine potato in large bowl
  with chicken, onion, spinach and
  half of the nuts; toss gently to
  combine. Drizzle with combined
  remaining ingredients. Serve
  sprinkled with remaining nuts.

SERVES 6
per serving 25.8g fat;
1965kJ (469 cal)
For a lower-fat version,
use light sour cream.
per serving 21.7g fat;
1828kJ (437 cal)

mexican bean potato salad

PREPARATION TIME 20 MINUTES (PLUS REFRIGERATION TIME) **COOKING TIME** 15 MINUTES

You can also use kipfler or ruby lou potatoes for this recipe.

1kg tiny new potatoes,
    unpeeled, quartered
1 tablespoon lime juice
2 tablespoons vegetable oil
⅓ cup (80g) sour cream
2 cloves garlic, crushed
300g can kidney beans,
    rinsed, drained
1 small red onion (100g),
    chopped finely
2 tablespoons finely chopped
    fresh flat-leaf parsley
2 tablespoons drained bottled
    sliced jalapeño chillies,
    chopped coarsely
1 small red capsicum (150g),
    chopped finely
1 large avocado (320g),
    chopped finely
1 cup loosely packed fresh
    coriander leaves
250g package corn tortillas

1 Boil, steam or microwave potato until just tender; drain. Cover; refrigerate 30 minutes.
2 Meanwhile, combine juice, oil, sour cream and garlic in screw-top jar; shake well. Combine beans, onion, parsley, chilli, capsicum, avocado and coriander in large bowl.
3 Add potato to bean mixture, pour dressing over salad; toss gently to combine. Serve with warmed tortillas.

SERVES 6
per serving 21.4g fat; 1757kJ (420 cal)
For a lower-fat version, use light sour cream.
per serving 18.7g fat; 1667kJ (398 cal)

balsamic potato salad

PREPARATION TIME 15 MINUTES (PLUS REFRIGERATION TIME) **COOKING TIME** 15 MINUTES

You can also use bintje or desiree potatoes for this recipe.

1kg pontiac potatoes, unpeeled, cut into wedges
6 green onions, sliced thinly
¼ cup (35g) drained sun-dried tomatoes, sliced thinly
½ cup (75g) seeded kalamata olives
½ cup (120g) sour cream
1 tablespoon balsamic vinegar
2 tablespoons milk
½ cup firmly packed fresh basil leaves

1 Boil, steam or microwave potato until just tender; drain. Cover; refrigerate 30 minutes.
2 Combine potato in large bowl with onion, tomato and olives.
3 Whisk sour cream, vinegar and milk in small bowl. Pour half of the dressing over salad; toss gently to combine. Add basil; toss gently to combine. Drizzle with remaining dressing.

SERVES 4
per serving 13.5g fat; 1375kJ (328 cal)

tuna and fennel potato salad

PREPARATION TIME 20 MINUTES **COOKING TIME** 40 MINUTES

Shallots, also called french shallots, golden shallots and eschalots, are not long-stemmed green onions but rather small, brown elongated members of the onion family. This recipes requires three 125g cans smoked tuna slices in springwater, but you can substitute an equivalent weight of any canned tuna you like.

1kg bintje potatoes, unpeeled, cut into wedges
⅓ cup (80ml) olive oil
3 baby fennel (390g), sliced thinly
1 tablespoon coarsely chopped fennel tips
¼ cup firmly packed fresh flat-leaf parsley leaves
2 tablespoons fresh tarragon leaves
¼ cup (50g) drained baby capers, rinsed
3 x 125g cans smoked tuna slices in springwater, drained, flaked
¼ cup (60ml) lemon juice
1 clove garlic, crushed

1 Preheat oven to moderately hot.
2 Place potato on lightly oiled oven tray; drizzle with 1 tablespoon of the oil. Roast in moderately hot oven about 40 minutes or until potato is browned lightly and tender. Cool 10 minutes.
3 Combine potato in large bowl with fennel, fennel tips, parsley, tarragon, capers and tuna.
4 Place remaining ingredients and remaining oil in screw-top jar; shake well. Pour dressing over salad; toss gently to combine.

SERVES 4
per serving 21.4g fat; 1874kJ (448 cal)

dill and caper potato salad

PREPARATION TIME 15 MINUTES **COOKING TIME** 15 MINUTES

You can also use pink fir apple or ruby lou potatoes for this recipe.

1kg tiny new potatoes,
   unpeeled, halved
2 tablespoons white
   wine vinegar
½ cup (125ml) olive oil
½ teaspoon sugar
1 teaspoon dijon mustard
⅓ cup (65g) drained
   baby capers
⅔ cup (140g) drained pickled
   cocktail onions, halved
1 cup (200g) drained cornichons,
   halved lengthways
2 tablespoons coarsely chopped
   fresh dill

1 Boil, steam or microwave potato
  until just tender; drain.
2 Meanwhile, combine vinegar, oil,
  sugar and mustard in screw-top
  jar; shake well.
3 Combine potato in large bowl
  with half of the dressing; cool
  10 minutes.
4 Add capers, onion, cornichon,
  dill and remaining dressing to
  salad; toss gently to combine.

SERVES 4
per serving 30.1g fat;
1929kJ (461 cal)

bintje
Oblong, smooth cream skin with shallow eyes, yellow flesh. Good for salads and frying.

coliban
Round, smooth white skin, white flesh. Good for baking and mashing.

desiree
Long and oval, smooth pink skin, creamy yellow flesh. Good for baking, roasting and in salads.

lasoda
Round, red skin with deep eyes, white flesh. Good for mashing and roasting.

nadine
Small and round, cream skin, white flesh. Good in salads.

nicola
Medium-sized and oval, beige skin, yellow flesh. Good for mashing.

purple congo
Elongated, purple skin with deep eyes, purple flesh. Good for frying.

ruby lou
Oval, dark pink skin with shallow eyes, white flesh. Good for roasting and in salads.

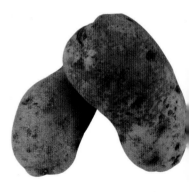

russet burbank
Long and oval, rough white skin with shallow eyes, white flesh. Good for baking and frying.

kennebec
Large and oval, light tan skin, white flesh. Good for frying.

king edward
Oval and kidney-shaped, pinky white skin, white flesh. Good for baking.

kipfler
Elongated and finger-shaped, yellow skin, yellow flesh. Good for roasting and in salads.

pink-eye
Medium-sized and round, white skin with pink around the eyes, white flesh. Good for mashing.

pink fir apple
Long and knobble-shaped, pink skin, yellow flesh. Good for roasting and in salads.

pontiac
Round, red skin with deep eyes, white flesh. Good for roasting and in salads.

sebago
Round, white skin with shallow eyes, white flesh. Good for mashing and baking.

spunta
Large and oblong, cream skin and yellow flesh. Good for baking and frying.

tiny new
Sometimes called chats; not a variety but just an early harvest. Small and round, white skin, white flesh. Good in salads.

glossary

almond meal also known as ground almonds; nuts are powdered to a coarse flour texture, for use in baking or as a thickener.

bacon rashers also known as bacon slices; made from cured and smoked pork.

bean

BROAD also known as fava, windsor or horse beans. Available dried, fresh or frozen, they are best if double-peeled, discarding both the outer long green pod and the beige-green tough inner shell.

KIDNEY medium-size red bean, slightly floury yet sweet in flavour; sold dried or canned.

besan a fine, powdery flour made from dried ground chickpeas; used throughout India for making various breads. Available from Asian supermarkets and health food stores.

bicarbonate of soda also known as baking soda; a common leavener.

breadcrumbs

PACKAGED crunchy, fine-textured, white breadcrumbs sold in supermarkets.

STALE one- or two-day-old bread made into crumbs by grating, blending or processing.

butter use salted or unsalted ("sweet") butter; 125g is equal to 1 stick butter.

buttermilk sold in the refrigerated dairy compartments in supermarkets. Originally just the liquid left after cream was separated from milk, today it is commercially made similarly to yogurt.

capers the grey-green buds of a warm climate (usually Mediterranean) shrub, sold either dried and salted or pickled in a vinegar brine. Baby capers are also available.

capsicum also known as bell pepper or, simply, pepper. Native to Central and South America, it can be red, green, yellow, orange or purplish black. Seeds and membranes should be discarded before use.

caster sugar also known as superfine or finely granulated table sugar.

celeriac root vegetable with brown skin, white flesh and celery-like flavour.

cheese

BLUE-VEIN mould-treated cheese mottled with blue veining. Varieties include firm and crumbly stilton types to mild, creamy brie-like cheeses.

FETTA Greek in origin; a crumbly textured goat- or sheep-milk cheese with a sharp, salty taste.

FONTINA a smooth, firm cheese with a nutty taste and a brown or red rind.

GOAT made from goat milk, has an earthy, strong taste; available in both soft and firm textures, in various shapes and sizes, sometimes rolled in ash or herbs.

GORGONZOLA a creamy Italian blue cheese having a mild, sweet taste; as good as an accompaniment to fruit as it is when used in cooking.

GRUYÈRE a Swiss cheese having small holes and a nutty, slightly salty flavour.

MASCARPONE a cultured cream product made in much the same way as yogurt. It is whitish to creamy yellow in colour, with a soft, creamy texture.

PIZZA a commercial blend of varying proportions of processed grated mozzarella, cheddar and parmesan.

PROVOLONE when young, similar to baby mozzarella; when aged is more pronounced in flavour and hard enough to grate.

RACLETTE a soft, sweet, good-melting Swiss cheese similar to emmental, gruyère and appenzeller. Also the name of a Swiss recipe similar to fondue where the cheese is melted and scooped up with cooked potatoes.

chillies

GREEN generally unripened thai chillies, but sometimes different varieties that are ripe when green, such as habanero, poblano or serrano chillies.

JALAPEÑO fairly hot green chillies, available in brine bottled or fresh from specialty greengrocers.

THAI, RED small, medium hot, and bright red in colour.

chorizo sausage a sausage of Spanish origin, made of coarsely ground pork and highly seasoned with garlic and chillies.

coriander also known as cilantro or chinese parsley when fresh; bright-green-leafed herb with a pungent flavour. Also sold as dried seeds or ground.

cornflour also known as cornstarch; used as a thickening agent in cooking.

cornichons French for gherkins, a very small variety of cucumber. Pickled, they are a traditional accompaniment to terrines and pâtés.

crème fraîche fresh, thick cream (minimum fat content 35%) having a velvety texture and tangy taste.

cucumber, lebanese short, thin-skinned and slender; this variety is also known as the european or burpless cucumber.

cumin also known as zeera or comino; resembling caraway in size, cumin is the dried seed of a plant related to the parsley family, having a spicy, nutty flavour. Available in seed form or dried and ground.

dijonnaise a commercially produced condiment that is a blend of dijon mustard and mayonnaise.

egg some recipes in this book call for raw or barely cooked eggs; exercise caution if there is a salmonella problem in your area.

eggplant purple-skinned vegetable also known as aubergine. Sold either raw or char-grilled and packed in oil.

food mill also known as a mouli; a rotary sieve used for liquidising and pureeing.

flour

PLAIN an all-purpose flour, made from wheat.

RICE a very fine flour, made from ground white rice.

SELF-RAISING plain flour sifted with baking powder in the proportion of 1 cup flour to 2 teaspoons baking powder.

garam masala a blend of spices, originating in North India; based on varying proportions of cardamom, cinnamon, cloves, coriander, fennel and cumin, roasted and ground together.

ghee clarified butter; when the milk solids are removed, the remaining fat can be heated to smoke point without burning.

ginger also known as green or root ginger; the thick, gnarled root of a tropical plant. Can be kept, peeled, covered with dry sherry in a jar and refrigerated, or frozen in an airtight container.

greek-style yogurt full-cream yogurt, often made from sheep milk; its thick, smooth consistency, almost like whipped cream, is attained by draining off the milk liquids. Good for making raitas and for use in cooking as well as eating on its own.

horseradish cream a creamy prepared paste of grated horseradish, vinegar, oil and sugar.

kumara Polynesian name of orange-fleshed sweet potato often confused with yam.

light cream we used cream with 18% fat.

light cream cheese we used cream cheese with 14% fat.

light mayonnaise we used cholesterol-free mayonnaise with 3% fat.

light sour cream we used light sour cream with 18.5% fat.

light yogurt we used yogurt with a fat content of less than 0.2%.

low-fat dairy-free spread we used a polyunsaturated, cholesterol-free, reduced-fat diet spread made of vegetable oils, water and gelatine, having 2.35g of fat per 5g.

mace similar to nutmeg in smell and taste, but more pungent. Typically sold in ground form.

mesclun an assortment of various edible green salad leaves.

mince meat also known as ground meat.

mirin sweet rice wine used in Japanese cooking; sometimes referred to simply as rice wine but not to be confused with sake, rice wine made for drinking.

oyster sauce Asian in origin, this rich, brown sauce is made from oysters and their brine, cooked with salt and soy sauce, and thickened with starches.

pancetta an Italian bacon that is spiced, then salt-cured, not smoked; flavourful and salty, it comes in a sausage-shaped roll and is sold sliced.

paprika ground dried red capsicum (bell pepper), available sweet or hot.

pine nuts also known as pignoli; not really nuts but small, cream-coloured kernels from the cones of several types of pine tree.

polenta also known as cornmeal; a flour-like cereal made of dried corn (maize) which is ground to three different textures: fine, medium or coarse. Polenta is also the name given to the Italian dish made from it.

potato ricer originally a German culinary tool, a ricer is a hand-operated sturdy press, usually made of stainless steel, which extrudes potatoes and other cooked vegetables through very fine holes.

prosciutto cured, air-dried (unsmoked), pressed ham; usually sold thinly sliced.

sambal oelek (also ulek or olek) Indonesian in origin; a salty paste made from ground chillies.

savoy cabbage a fairly bland, large head with crinkled dark-green outer leaves.

sichuan peppercorns also known as szechuan or chinese pepper, a mildly hot spice that comes from the prickly ash tree. Although not related to the peppercorn family, sichuan berries look like black peppercorns and have a distinctively peppery-lemon flavour and aroma.

snow pea tendrils the growing shoots of the snow pea plant; sold by greengrocers and most supermarkets. The succulent stems and leaves can be stir-fried, steamed or eaten raw in salads.

star anise a star-shaped, dried pod whose seeds have an astringent aniseed flavour; used to flavour stocks and marinades.

sumac a purple-red, astringent spice ground from berries growing on shrubs that flourish wild around the Mediterranean. It adds a tart, lemony flavour to both cooked and raw foods.

tomato

EGG also called plum or roma, these are smallish and oval-shaped.

RELISH sometimes called tomato chutney; commercial condiment made from tomatoes, onions, vinegar and various spices.

SAUCE also known as ketchup or catsup; a flavoured condiment made from slow-cooked tomatoes, vinegar and spices.

SEMI-DRIED partially dried tomato sections, usually sold marinated in herbed olive oil.

tortilla thin, round unleavened bread which originated in Mexico; can be made at home or purchased vacuum-packed, frozen or fresh. Two kinds are available, one made from wheat flour and the other from corn (maize meal).

vinegar

APPLE CIDER made from fermented apples.

BALSAMIC authentic only from the province of Modena, Italy; made from a regional wine of white Trebbiano grapes specially processed, then aged in antique wooden casks to give an exquisite pungent flavour.

RICE WINE made from fermented rice, colourless and flavoured with sugar and salt. Also known as seasoned rice vinegar.

v-slicer a classic German kitchen tool used for slicing, shredding, dicing and julienning of fruits and vegetables; prized for its speed and precision.

wasabi an Asian horseradish used to make the pungent, green-coloured sauce traditionally served with Japanese raw fish dishes; sold in powdered or paste form.

zucchini also known as courgette, belonging to the squash family.

make your own stock

These recipes can be made up to four days ahead and stored, covered, in the refrigerator. Be sure to remove any fat from the surface after the cooled stock has been refrigerated overnight. If the stock is to be kept longer, it is best to freeze it in smaller quantities. *All stock recipes make about 2.5 litres (10 cups).*

Stock is also available in cans or cartons. Stock cubes or powder can be used. As a guide, 1 teaspoon of stock powder or 1 small crumbled stock cube mixed with 1 cup (250ml) water will give a fairly strong stock. Be aware of the salt and fat content of stock cubes and powders and prepared stocks.

BEEF STOCK

2kg meaty beef bones
2 medium onions (300g)
2 sticks celery, chopped
2 medium carrots (250g), chopped
3 bay leaves
2 teaspoons black peppercorns
5 litres (20 cups) water
3 litres (12 cups) water, extra

Place bones and unpeeled chopped onions in baking dish; bake in hot oven about 1 hour or until bones and onions are well browned. Transfer bones and onions to large saucepan, add celery, carrots, bay leaves, peppercorns and the water; simmer, uncovered, 3 hours. Add extra water; simmer, uncovered, 1 hour. Strain.

CHICKEN STOCK

2kg chicken bones
2 medium onions (300g), chopped
2 sticks celery, chopped
2 medium carrots (250g), chopped
3 bay leaves
2 teaspoons black peppercorns
5 litres (20 cups) water

Combine ingredients in large saucepan; simmer, uncovered, 2 hours. Strain.

VEGETABLE STOCK

2 large carrots (360g), chopped
2 large parsnips (360g), chopped
4 medium onions (600g), chopped
12 sticks celery, chopped
4 bay leaves
2 teaspoons black peppercorns
6 litres (24 cups) water

Combine ingredients in large saucepan; simmer, uncovered, 1½ hours. Strain.

index

facts + figures

Wherever you live, you'll be able to use our recipes with the help of these easy-to-follow conversions. While these conversions are approximate only, the difference between an exact and the approximate conversion of various liquid and dry measures is but minimal and will not affect your cooking results.

dry measures

metric	imperial
15g	½oz
30g	1oz
60g	2oz
90g	3oz
125g	4oz (¼lb)
155g	5oz
185g	6oz
220g	7oz
250g	8oz (½lb)
280g	9oz
315g	10oz
345g	11oz
375g	12oz (¾lb)
410g	13oz
440g	14oz
470g	15oz
500g	16oz (1lb)
750g	24oz (1½lb)
1kg	32oz (2lb)

liquid measures

metric	imperial
30ml	1 fluid oz
60ml	2 fluid oz
100ml	3 fluid oz
125ml	4 fluid oz
150ml	5 fluid oz (¼ pint/1 gill)
190ml	6 fluid oz
250ml	8 fluid oz
300ml	10 fluid oz (½ pint)
500ml	16 fluid oz
600ml	20 fluid oz (1 pint)
1000ml (1 litre)	1¾ pints

helpful measures

metric	imperial
3mm	⅛in
6mm	¼in
1cm	½in
2cm	¾in
2.5cm	1in
5cm	2in
6cm	2½in
8cm	3in
10cm	4in
13cm	5in
15cm	6in
18cm	7in
20cm	8in
23cm	9in
25cm	10in
28cm	11in
30cm	12in (1ft)

measuring equipment

The difference between one country's measuring cups and another's is, at most, within a 2 or 3 teaspoon variance. (For the record, 1 Australian metric measuring cup holds approximately 250ml.) The most accurate way of measuring dry ingredients is to weigh them. When measuring liquids, use a clear glass or plastic jug with the metric markings. (One Australian metric tablespoon holds 20ml; one Australian metric teaspoon holds 5ml.)

If you would like to purchase The Australian Women's Weekly Test Kitchen's metric measuring cups and spoons (as approved by Standards Australia), turn to page 120 for details and order coupon. You will receive:

■ a graduated set of four cups for measuring dry ingredients, with sizes marked on the cups.

■ a graduated set of four spoons for measuring dry and liquid ingredients, with amounts marked on the spoons.

Note: North America, NZ and the UK use 15ml tablespoons. All cup and spoon measurements are level.

We use large eggs having an average weight of 60g.

how to measure

When using graduated metric measuring cups, shake dry ingredients loosely into the appropriate cup. Do not tap the cup on a bench or tightly pack the ingredients unless directed to do so. Level top of measuring cups and measuring spoons with a knife. When measuring liquids, place a clear glass or plastic jug with metric markings on a flat surface to check accuracy at eye level.

oven temperatures

These oven temperatures are only a guide. Always check the manufacturer's manual.

	°C (Celsius)	°F (Fahrenheit)	Gas Mark
Very slow	120	250	1
Slow	150	300	2
Moderately slow	160	325	3
Moderate	180 – 190	350 – 375	4
Moderately hot	200 – 210	400 – 425	5
Hot	220 – 230	450 – 475	6
Very hot	240 – 250	500 – 525	7

Looking after **your interest...**

Keep your ACP cookbooks clean, tidy and within easy reach with slipcovers designed to hold up to 12 books. Plus you can follow our recipes perfectly with a set of accurate measuring cups and spoons, as used by *The Australian Women's Weekly* Test Kitchen.

To order

Mail or fax Photocopy and complete the coupon below and post to ACP Books Reader Offer, ACP Publishing, GPO Box 4967, Sydney NSW 2001, or fax to (02) 9267 4967.

Phone Have your credit card details ready, then phone 136 116 (Mon-Fri, 8.00am-6.00pm; Sat, 8.00am-6.00pm).

Price

Book Holder

Australia: $13.10 (incl. GST).
Elsewhere: $A21.95.

Metric Measuring Set

Australia: $6.50 (incl. GST).
New Zealand: $8.00.
Elsewhere: $A9.95.

Prices include postage and handling. This offer is available in all countries.

Payment

Australian residents

We accept the credit cards listed on the coupon, money orders and cheques.

Overseas residents

We accept the credit cards listed on the coupon, drafts in $A drawn on an Australian bank, and also British, New Zealand and U.S. cheques in the currency of the country of issue. Credit card charges are at the exchange rate current at the time of payment.

Photocopy and complete coupon below

- -

☐ **Book Holder**

☐ **Metric Measuring Set**
Please indicate number(s) required.

Mr/Mrs/Ms _____

Address _____

_____

Postcode _____ Country _____

Ph: Business hours ( ) _____

I enclose my cheque/money order for $ _____ payable to ACP Publishing.

OR: please charge my

☐ Bankcard ☐ Visa ☐ Mastercard

☐ Diners Club ☐ American Express

| | | | | | | | | | | | | | | | | |

Card number

Expiry date ____ /____

Cardholder's signature _____

Please allow up to 30 days delivery within Australia.
Allow up to 6 weeks for overseas deliveries.
Both offers expire 31/12/04. HLP03

Test Kitchen Staff
Food director *Pamela Clark*
Food editor *Karen Hammial*
Assistant food editor *Amira Ibram*
Test Kitchen manager *Kimberley Coverdale*
Home economists *Belinda Black,*
Sammie Coryton, Kelly Cruickshanks,
Cathie Lonnie, Christina Martignago,
Jeanette Seamons, Jessica Sly,
Kate Tait, Alison Webb
Editorial coordinator *Rebecca Steyns*

ACP Books Staff
Editorial director *Susan Tomnay*
Creative director *Hieu Chi Nguyen*
Senior editor *Lynda Wilton*
Designer *Alison Windmill*
Studio manager *Caryl Wiggins*
Editorial coordinator *Caroline Lowry*
Editorial assistant *Karen Lai*
Publishing manager (sales) *Brian Cearnes*
Publishing manager (rights & new projects)
Jane Hazell
Brand manager *Donna Gianniotis*
Pre-press *Harry Palmer*
Production manager *Carol Currie*
Business manager *Sally Lees*

Chief executive officer *John Alexander*
Group publisher *Jill Baker*
Publisher *Sue Wannan*

Produced by ACP Books, Sydney.

Printed by Dai Nippon Printing in Korea.
Published by ACP Publishing Pty Limited,
54 Park St, Sydney; GPO Box 4088,
Sydney, NSW 2001.
Ph: (02) 9282 8618 Fax: (02) 9267 9438.
acpbooks@acp.com.au
www.acpbooks.com.au

To order books, phone 136 116.
Send recipe enquiries to:
recipeenquiries@acp.com.au

AUSTRALIA: Distributed by Network Services
GPO Box 4088, Sydney, NSW 2001.
Ph: (02) 9282 8777 Fax: (02) 9264 3278.

UNITED KINGDOM: Distributed by Australian
Consolidated Press (UK), Moulton Park
Business Centre, Red House Rd,
Moulton Park, Northampton, NN3 6AQ.
Ph: (01604) 497 531 Fax: (01604) 497 533
acpukltd@aol.com

CANADA: Distributed by Whitecap Books Ltd
351 Lynn Ave, North Vancouver, BC, V7J 2C4.
Ph: (604) 980 9852 Fax: (604) 980 8197
customerservice@whitecap.ca
www.whitecap.ca

NEW ZEALAND: Distributed by Netlink
Distribution Company, ACP Media Centre,
Cnr Fanshawe and Beaumont Streets,
Westhaven, Auckland.
PO Box 47906, Ponsonby, Auckland, NZ.
Ph: (9) 366 9966 ask@ndcnz.co.nz

Clark, Pamela.
The Australian Women's Weekly
Potatoes.

Includes index.
ISBN 1 86396 303 0
1. Cookery (Potatoes). I. Title. II. Title:
Australian Women's Weekly.
641.6521

© ACP Publishing Pty Limited 2003
ABN 18 053 273 546

The publishers would like to thank
Major & Tom, St Peters, NSW, for props
used in photography.